The Heart of a High School

One Community's Effort to Transform Urban Education

Holly Holland & Kelly Mazzoli

HEINEMANN
Portsmouth, NH

Heinemann
A division of Reed Elsevier Inc.
361 Hanover Street
Portsmouth, NH 03801–3912
www.heinemann.com

Offices and agents throughout the world

Copublished by the Stark Education Partnership, 220 Market Avenue South, Suite 350
Canton, Ohio 44702-2171; 330-452-0829

Library of Congress Cataloging-in-Publication Data
CIP data is on file with the Library of Congress.
ISBN 0-325-00393-9

Editor: Lois Bridges
Copyediting: Laurel Robinson Editorial Services, Machias, Maine
Interior and cover design: Katie Sullivan, Flossmoor, Illinois
Photography: Todd Rosenberg Photography, Chicago
Manufacturing: Louise Richardson

Printed in the United States of America on acid-free paper

05   04   03   02   01   DA   1   2   3   4   5

*To the public school teachers represented in this book
and to those teachers everywhere who strive daily
to fulfill the promise of education reform*

CONTENTS

PREFACE

At ten o'clock in the morning on the first day of high school, August 24, 1999, hundreds of freshmen dutifully filed into the sweeping auditorium for a mandatory orientation session. Teenagers and teachers looked each other over and surreptitiously commented on the conspicuous parade.

One teacher pointed out a kid who was repeating his freshman year for the third time. "Can you imagine?" she asked, and shook her head sadly. "He'll be the oldest freshman alive."

Another student nudged the person next to him: "Oh, my God, that's Amanda," he said. "She must have flunked. See that blonde over there? She flunked, too."

The hubbub ceased as Clifton Rush, the imposing, barrel-chested principal of Abraham Lincoln High School, walked to the stage. Seated to his right were five assistant administrators who stared soberly at the crowd.

"May we have your attention, please?" Rush spoke into the microphone, his baritone voice needing no amplification. "Welcome to the Class of 2003. We are happy you chose Lincoln. We are proud not of our tradition but of you as students. There is no Lincoln without you, the students. We're here to serve you as you choose your future."

With that, he introduced his assistants, identifying the four men and one woman according to the student alphabet pool — Leech to Oswald, Otto to Sew — that he or she would be responsible for guiding during the coming year. The regimented sorting process, so endemic to the organization of the modern American high school, was already under way.

"Take a look around at the person next to you," Rush commanded. "I hope to see you all here at the end of the year."

With that, the pleasantries ended. Rush left the stage and each of his assistants took a turn at the podium. One by one, they described "the rules" by which order would be maintained. "We don't tolerate ignorance," an angry, white-haired man thundered to the masses. "You, in the orange. You got a problem? Then listen."

He outlined the various ways students could get suspended or expelled, described the canine unit that would sniff for drugs in lockers and parked cars — "Pagers, we see 'em or hear 'em, we take 'em" — and mentioned the "uniformed" police officer who would patrol the building throughout the year. "If you're caught smoking, we will get you. We will suspend you."

After several short speeches about the school's new Safety Hot Line — which parents or citizens can call to anonymously report students suspected of using drugs — the student dress code, the laminated identification cards each teenager would be required to wear around the neck at all times, and the method for requesting changes in "the schedule," the administrator changed subjects.

"Now, football tickets," he said, smiling for the first time. He then proceeded to explain how freshmen could, indeed must, contribute to Lincoln High's school spirit.

"I hope to see most of you next year when we do sophomore orientation," another administrator announced without enthusiasm at the end of the presentation. "But that's up to you. Do what you're supposed to. Follow the rules. Remember, we're here to help you."

As the future leaders of Gladston, U.S.A., were leaving the auditorium, one skeptical student turned to her teacher and asked, "Aren't we supposed to have fun and enjoy learning?"

It was a good question. But the answer depends on which high school the student asking it happens to attend. For many American teenagers, learning is not pleasurable, personal, or relevant. High schools are set up to accommodate adult schedules and preferences and rarely take into account students' interests, needs, or concerns. As early as the ninth grade, many students discover that it's futile to follow the drill. They tune out, drop out, and in a few tragic cases, shoot their way out.

This book examines some of the reasons why. It steps inside the classrooms, the homes, and the heads of high school students to find out why some fail to reach the destination of learning. It spends time with their teachers to discover why some frequently connect with today's teenagers and why some never do. And it examines the attitudes and institutional barriers that keep many promising practices from spreading beyond a single classroom or school. Although this narrative focuses on one industrial city in one Midwestern state, it's really the story of an American institution in desperate need of repair.

As William Glasser writes in *The Quality School Teacher*, "It is necessary to face the fact that a majority of students, even good ones, believe that much of the present academic curriculum is not worth the effort it takes to learn it. The answer is not to make them work harder; it is to increase the quality of what we ask them to learn."

In the spring of 1999, we were hired by a nonprofit civic organization in Gladston to report on the progress of a public school reform initiative known as the Jefferson Regional Campus project. Although more complex than this brief summary suggests, the project essentially aims to reposition the city's "bad" public high school, Thomas Jefferson, a faded comprehensive high school and vocational center, as a world class education hub. In the process, the school district also hopes to change the culture of its other high school — Lincoln — the popular and widely perceived "good" school, which shares its athletic stadium with Gladston's tourist mecca, a pro sports museum.

However, this education reform initiative, like so many others around the country, suffers from a lack of agreement both inside and outside the system about the need to fix either school. Many educators and citizens of the community continue to deny the glaring problems, including high dropout and suspension rates, poor to mediocre standardized test scores, and absenteeism so unmanageable that many teachers don't know — and some don't care — who shows up for class each day.

Gladston's school leaders have been trying to come up with a plan to fix Jefferson High School for almost two decades. The idea of developing a downtown campus that would offer a range of educational opportunities to students came from a group of citizens who convened at the request of Superintendent Lyndon LaGrange. Later, another local group chaired by Michael Rutherford, president of Monument State College of Technology, began meeting to figure out how to bring this Jefferson Regional Campus idea to reality. And in 1996, the Gladston Professional Educators Association, which represents the city's public school teachers, proposed a series of academies focusing on different career paths students could choose to follow. All of these efforts coalesced in 1997 when the Davidsons, Gladston's leading family and scions of an international industrial conglomerate, pledged $10 million to resurrect the high school that they built for the city sixty years ago. The money suddenly turned these interrelated pipe dreams into real possibilities.

"We don't know if this will work, but we know they'll never have another chance like this," said John Williams "Will" Davidson, president of the Davidson Foundation of Gladston and the person who initiated what is believed to be one of the largest private donations ever awarded to a single public school. "If we have the guts to try something different in this community, we can make a difference."

For Davidson, who also sits on the board of the nonprofit group monitoring the implementation of the $10 million grant, money can be a wedge to open the closeted community of public education. Davidson believes that if he can help shake up the bureaucracy of the Gladston school district so that it demonstrates real progress in student achievement, he can show his community that vouchers and charter schools are not just the work of extremists but the beginning of a movement of citizens who no longer will tolerate mediocrity in public education.

"The school system is afraid of competition, and they have developed a sort of black hat and white hat mentality that change is evil. To me, that is wrong," Davidson said. "Our school system isn't great. We've been told it's great.... But what bothers me is that I can't hire half the kids in this community because they're not qualified."

The Gladston story is important from a national perspective because it involves so many perplexing issues in education today: how to define and meet higher academic standards, how to help teachers and students understand the changing educational requirements of the new world economy, and how to counteract the corrosive effects of urban poverty. Billions of dollars have been spent on education reform initiatives across the country in the last two decades. Although there have been some modest successes, no one is ready to say, "That's a wrap" and call it a day. Too many problems remain.

Individual teachers and individual schools around the country have succeeded in making learning rigorous, relevant, and rewarding for all the students they serve, not just the ones who come from educated and supportive families. But these success stories are by no means universal. Although research has identified the qualities of excellent schools — including high expectations for teaching and learning, a well-designed curriculum that builds sequentially, and continuing education for teachers — communities repeatedly have failed to develop these characteristics in all public schools. As a result, education reform continues to be the hope of many and the reality of a few.

Which path will Gladston choose? The journey begins inside.

— Holly Holland and Kelly Mazzoli

ACKNOWLEDGEMENTS

Writing and publishing a work of nonfiction depends to a large extent on the guidance, assistance, and cooperation of key characters in the story. Many people in the Gladston community gave generously of their time and talents to help us tell others about their experiences with school reform. We are grateful for their hospitality, their openness, and their faith in our ability to accurately share their stories.

Although all of the events described in the book are true, we changed the names of the community and the participants so we could write the most honest portrayal without subjecting anyone to direct criticism. The only exception to this practice is Judy Hummel, a senior associate at the Center for Leadership in School Reform in Louisville, Kentucky, whose name appears throughout the book. Because Judy works with so many schools and school districts around the country, her connection to Gladston will not inadvertently reveal the community's identity. We thank Judy for her unfailing honesty and goodwill during the reporting process and for her willingness to be named and portrayed in the book.

In addition to changing the names of everyone else in the book, we had to dispense with using formal citations for some references, such as the local newspaper, whose inclusion would have quickly revealed Gladston's actual name. From the beginning, we intended for this work to be instructive to Gladston and any other community that undertakes major school reform. By its nature, change is difficult and messy, a process that often reveals personalities and actions that are neither flattering nor positive. Because change in the education arena usually occurs under the glare of the public spotlight, ordinary tensions and anxieties escalate even more. We did not wish to add to the pressure. We hoped only to reveal the inner workings of secondary education so that a wider audience of educators and policymakers could use the information to examine and adjust their own practices for the benefit of students.

We extend special thanks to the staff of the Gladston education partnership for coordinating our visits to the community and supporting our research there. Executive Director Martin Diego was a forceful advocate who shepherded our work and protected the independence of our evaluation from the start. We also are deeply grateful to the staff and students at the freshman academy and the business academy for giving us complete access to their schools and for revealing the full range of their joys and frustrations during the first year of an ambitious educational agenda. Never did these individuals shut us out of meetings or deprive us of requested information. To the contrary, they responded helpfully to all of our inquiries so we could get a fuller picture of the lives of high school students and teachers.

We had hoped that writer Audrey Chapman would play a larger role in the book than she did. After reporting some key events in the Gladston story and interviewing some of the participants, Audrey was involved in a serious car accident that kept her from working for almost a year. We missed her keen observations and strong narrative voice, but we are glad to know that she has healed.

We followed the development of the Jefferson Regional Campus project from the spring of 1999 through the fall of 2000, with special emphasis on the 1999–2000 school year. We spent hundreds of hours interviewing and observing educators, students, parents, and various citizens of Gladston. The events in this book are based on our observations or recreated with help from the participants. Although we made every effort to verify dates, identify responsible parties, and clarify the chronological sequence of events, we had to rely on published reports and participants' personal memories that sometimes presented conflicting information. All history is subject to interpretation; the Gladston story is no different.

If you wish to contact the participants or comment on the book, please send us a note and we will forward your request/feedback to the appropriate people to see if they would like to get in touch with you. For Holly Holland: hollyholland@mindspring.com or 4004 Alton Road, Louisville, KY 40207. For Kelly Mazzoli:kellymazzoli@mindspring. com or 901 Hampshire Drive, Louisville, KY 40207. For Heinemann: Go to www.heinemann.com and look for contact information.

PART I

The Cult of High School

I

JEFFERSON HIGH SCHOOL

"Large public institutions are not designed for adaptability. They are like freight trains moving down a single track. They cannot change direction or stop easily. Some say that only by building a new railroad can the needed change come about."

— *Davidson Regional Campus Project*
Comprehensive Progress Report
January 1999

When the Davidson Foundation gave the Gladston school district $1,300,000 in 1937 to create a world-class vocational school, it was thinking of economic as well as community interests. Like many other industrial businesses that expanded in the years after the Great Depression, the Davidson Company needed skilled machinists, electricians, welders, and other craftsmen to work in its sprawling plants throughout the region. But the school system didn't offer the right training for the available jobs.

"Gladston is one of the most highly industrialized cities in the country, which means that most boys graduating from the Gladston High Schools must go into the factories in that vicinity if they expect to reside in Fulkerson County," T. L. Davidson, the son of the company's founder, wrote in 1938. "There is not one first class vocational high school in" the state. "We hope to create one."

Ironically, Lincoln High School had started a vocational program two years earlier. But in an early sign of the rivalry between the two schools that would rage for more than half a century, business leaders decided that the existing program wasn't good enough. They wanted to develop one of their own.

Gladston's industrialists weren't alone in their desire to adjust the high school curriculum to support their hiring and training needs. The push for more practical studies in high schools occurred in communities throughout the country as teenagers who in previous generations would have left school after the elementary grades began swelling secondary enrollments. The ensuing debate about the importance of traditional academic versus vocational courses in secondary education has continued to this day: What should a basic high school education include? Are all students capable of mastering it? Should schools sort students by their perceived abilities, preparing less capable graduates for work and more elite graduates for college? Should course offerings be changed to suit shifting social priorities, or should the requirements for a high school diploma remain a constant standard by which we can judge the quality of future generations?

The inability to adequately address these questions is among our greatest failures as a society. Indeed, education reform might one day become known as the second Hundred Years War, a series of sporadic conflicts that ended with no one scoring a decisive victory.

As David L. Angus and Jeffery E. Mirel note in their book *The Failed Promise of the American High School 1890–1995*, educators have claimed throughout the twentieth century that each subsequent wave of secondary students was more poorly suited for intellectual work than the previous generation. In 1904, one leading educator referred to the new students as a "great army of incapables...who should be in schools for dullards or subnormal children." In 1925, an assistant superintendent of a large urban school district claimed that a third of high school students were "congenitally incapable of doing high school work as it is now constituted." By 1940, the point at which Gladston's business leaders were trying to create a new high school model, the descriptions had changed very little. First-generation high school students were considered to be "dull" and having "poor mental equipment."[1]

Educators used this argument again in the 1950s as American high schools came under increasing attack for their weak intellectual underpinnings. When people charged that neither the life skills courses favored for children from working class homes nor the college-preparatory programs for students from the professional classes were rigorous enough, educators called the critics "cranks" and "enemies of the public schools."[2]

The rhetorical fusillade resulted in a greater reinforcement of the "system" and a growing tendency of educators to consider all critiques to be the work of agitators unfamiliar with the difficult job of teaching the masses. The comprehensive high school, with its highly stratified, cafeteria-style offerings, thus continued with little interruption.

"Without a doubt, the period between 1950 and 1975 was one in which a variety of critics directly challenged the educational status quo, and controversies about the high school curriculum intensified," Angus and Mirel write. "Despite those controversies, however, we find that the course-taking patterns of American high school students actually changed very little. Indeed, during this period the core beliefs of educational professionals — that most high school students were incapable of doing rigorous academic work, that curriculum differentiation was the key to equality of educational opportunity, and that the high school was primarily a custodial institution — gained even greater influence than before."[3]

With this backdrop, the early success of the new Jefferson Vocational High School owed much to the political and economic power wielded by Gladston's leading industrialists. Working behind the scenes, Davidson's representatives and school leaders determined that the next great thrust for secondary education must be in vocational training that was tied directly to local employment patterns. Building on business reports of the industrial occupations with the highest expected growth rates, they developed an extensive curriculum for the new high school.

Now all they lacked was a building to put it in. They decided to raze the old Central High School, in the heart of downtown Gladston. The Davidson Company not only gave money to the school district for a new vocational high school, but also supervised the entire project.

"The building went up in 186 working days — possible only because the construction was handled by the Davidson Company, thus avoiding the legislative delays that would have occurred had it been built by the school board," according to an account published by the local historical society. "The financing and purchasing were all done through the Davidson purchasing department…. The final cost was $950,000 for building and $300,000 for equipment, all paid for by the Davidson Foundation."

The imposing five-story building — made of structural steel and reinforced concrete, brick, and sandstone — opened in the fall of 1939 with 1,400 students. The first night of a planned three-day open house drew 6,000 people from the community.

Over the next two decades, Jefferson Vocational High School produced a steady stream of tradesmen and office workers for local industries. In a matriculation pattern similar to the vocational emphasis of the proposed Jefferson Regional Campus academy concept, students first explored different careers, then developed vocational specialties and spent part of the school day working as apprentices for the companies that would later hire them full time.

"For fifty years, Jefferson High School served our community precisely as it was intended," wrote the chairman of the school's fiftieth anniversary celebration in 1989. "When it focused on vocational curricula, students were provided with practical learning opportunities that eased the transition from classroom to workplace."

In 1955, the high school adopted a selective admissions policy based on standardized test scores, vocational aptitude, and grades. And until the early 1980s, "the school was a model of excellence in vocational education," Superintendent Lyndon LaGrange wrote in a funding proposal to the state in 1997. "Then, to address changing times and population patterns, the school was transformed into a standard comprehensive high school. Subsequent years saw urban blight and all of the emerging problems of urban secondary education take their toll on the proud tradition of the school and negatively affect the citizens of our community in terms of economic power."

LaGrange's narrative does not mention the decisions made by the Gladston Board of Education that seemed to exacerbate the problems at Jefferson. In 1976, for example, Jefferson became a "comprehensive high school." The school system updated its vocational options and began offering a stronger academic program at Jefferson.

High-achieving students were attracted to the school's college preparatory courses, including a wide array of Advanced Placement classes, which enable students to earn college credit for their work if they attain certain scores on qualifying exams. At the same time, the school district converted two of the city's four high schools to junior highs and moved Lincoln from its downtown location to a spacious new campus near the edge of the city's boundary with more affluent and sprawling suburban communities.

James Dawson, superintendent of the Gladston schools at the time, had wanted to build the new Lincoln campus downtown. But the school board, under pressure from downtown merchants who didn't want teenagers hanging around their businesses, overturned Dawson's decision. During the next decade, many of the influential merchants made certain that no teenagers would hang around when they closed their downtown stores for good.

Under the reorganization of Gladston's secondary education program in 1976, the school board closed Grant and Harding high schools and rebuilt the curricula at Jefferson and

Lincoln. The two remaining high schools were to offer similar basic courses but develop different academic specialties. Lincoln would take over three of the school district's twenty-eight vocational programs — carpentry, food service, and printing — and concentrate on advanced academic courses in the humanities. Jefferson would keep the remaining twenty-five vocational programs and expand its advanced math and science classes. While Jefferson kept the more traditional advanced math and science classes, Lincoln was to offer a different lineup of courses aimed at students who might not choose careers in fields such as engineering that require intensive preparation in the hard sciences. Instead, Lincoln adopted an approach that integrated math and science concepts through broad topics that sought to remove the artificial boundaries between algebra and geometry, for example, or chemistry and biology.

Graduates and faculty members remember 1976 as the final golden age for Jefferson when large numbers of students won scholarships to prestigious universities and the high school was renowned for its math team, student newspaper, speech and debate team, and drama presentations. Jefferson's enrollment stood at 1,900, higher than Lincoln's. Within a few years, however, Jefferson lost almost every edge it once had over its crosstown rival. Its enrollment dropped 42 percent from 1976 to 1992.

Structurally, there is no comparison between the two high schools. Lincoln shares a stadium with the pro sports museum. It has a performing arts hall, a natatorium, huge gymnasium and weight-training facilities, modern classrooms, and ample parking. Jefferson's grand façade suddenly looked as outdated as the downtown department stores that were being vacated all over the country as customers started flocking to the mammoth, one-story commercial chains sprouting in suburban shopping malls. Jefferson doesn't have central air conditioning or carpeting. Its cafeteria is on the fifth floor, and its dreary, windowless gymnasium is on the third floor, with worn, splintered seating and no easy access for spectators. To get to Jefferson's football practice field, a tarnished dime compared with Lincoln's shiny silver dollar, players have to hike two city blocks through downtown traffic.

The real clincher occurred after the 1976–1977 school year when parents of Lincoln's students began pressuring the school board to give their children the same advanced math and science courses that had made Jefferson a sound choice for top students. At the time, students who wanted to take the designated Advanced Placement math and science classes had to have a B average and a teacher's recommendation, but the courses were available only at Jefferson. Although Lincoln educators believed that their integrated math and science courses were just as rigorous as the traditional Advanced Placement courses at Jefferson, they had a difficult time persuading parents and college administrators that the courses were the same. Jerome Katz, who served as Lincoln's principal from 1976 to 1979, said some parents were concerned that if their children's high school transcripts included courses such as Unified Math instead of the more traditional Algebra II and Calculus, for example, they would not be evaluated in the most positive light. By the end of the decade, he said, the pendulum had swung back and the two schools offered the same high-level courses.

"Once they duplicated the courses, the floodgates opened," Superintendent LaGrange said in an interview.

Jefferson started bleeding from every artery. As it steadily lost students to Lincoln, the school struggled to get enough students to field the football team and the marching band. The numbers of students in introductory and remedial classes soared, and fewer students enrolled in advanced math and science courses each year. The student poverty rate rose — it was 53 percent during the 1999–2000 school year, according to information provided by Jefferson High School — as property values in the neighborhoods surrounding the school declined. Attendance problems, discipline referrals, dropouts, suspensions — every indicator of the school's overall health worsened.

Nolan Stevens, Jefferson's principal from 1977 to 1982 and superintendent of the Gladston schools from 1983 to 1989, said faculty members and school district administrators were slow to realize how much the high school had declined. He said some resisted even the minor modifications attempted at Jefferson in the 1980s, such as trying to do a better job of relating the required academic content to the students' chosen vocational courses.

"There were attempts made, and I can't say that any of them were extremely successful," Stevens said. "We were always like on the edge of things but couldn't quite" turn the situation around…. "There was a lot of resistance to change, I guess."

A 1999 progress report on the Jefferson Regional Campus project put it more bluntly: "…for the most part the changes have been attempts to keep pace with huge changes in the rest of the world by making small adjustments in course work and equipment."

As the final decade of the twentieth century dawned, the signs of trouble were piling up as steadily as patients at a hospital triage desk. Jefferson High School was in critical condition. And like the transplant patient waiting for a lifesaving donation, the once-vigorous institution hung on in hopes that some miraculous intervention might restore it to health.

2

"WE CAN'T GET THEM TO COME TO SCHOOL"

One girl said she couldn't resist the temptation to walk out a side door when she was changing classes in the middle of the school day.

Another girl, an honors student in eighth grade, missed 101 days during her freshman year because, she said, she had developed a phobia of school.

Other students said they slept in and skipped classes because their parents were at work, or didn't care or, well, just because.

Some of these students will end up at Transitions, an alternative school operated by the Gladston district in collaboration with five other school districts in the county. Some of them will get low-paying jobs, get pregnant, or go to jail. And some of them will show up the following school year, another year older, another year behind, and one step closer to dropping out for good.

Administrators at Jefferson High School spend the better part of each weekday trying to keep approximately 1,100 students inside the eight different buildings that make up the eleven-block downtown campus. With many teenagers, they don't succeed. In a typical year, according to Gladston school district figures, about one in five Jefferson students will fail for the year and one in six will drop out. In addition, during the 1999–2000 school year, Jefferson students were suspended 995 times (some students had multiple infractions), and seventy-five students were expelled.

"I basically just left out the front door. They got so many buildings and so many doors, that's a real problem," explained Ashley, a sixteen-year-old freshman who said she started skipping detention and then skipping school altogether after an altercation with a teacher who was supervising an in-school suspension class. She said she's making much better progress at Transitions because of the small class sizes and the intensive mediation from teachers and counselors.

"For me it's better because when I'm at Jefferson I always end up with the wrong crowd. I'm always doing something stupid," she said. "The teachers always, I mean, they'll help you with your work, but sometimes they just give it to you. They tell you something, but they don't explain it until you understand. But here, you know, they sit down and make sure you know what you're doing."

Roderick Johnson, an assistant principal who has spent

two decades at Jefferson, acknowledged that the measures the school has adopted to keep track of students go only so far in keeping them in class and out of trouble.

"It's not like your regular school," he acknowledged. "I mean, it's a true campus-type of setup, which is nice in college, but difficult here." In a given year, 500-600 hundred kids "come in and go out because of the mobility [rates] of the inner city. So probably in the course of any given year, we deal with over two thousand students here…. That's a lot of paperwork, a lot of changing schedules."

Using an elaborate check-in system, Jefferson's staff first requires students to run their laminated photo identification cards through an electronic scanner in the main entrance to the school. Teachers then verify attendance during the first-period classes and send lists of absent students to the office for another check against the official enrollment sheet. A gun-toting police officer and a crew of security guards also roam the halls — the school employs more than twice as many building monitors as counselors — and the crackle of walkie-talkies is as constant as the drone of the classroom lectures on every floor. Twenty-three closed-circuit television cameras observe all the movements throughout the main school building.

But as regimented as the check-in policy is at Jefferson High School, the check-out practices vary as widely as a teenager's imagination. The school nurse often sees dozens of students a day, many of whom just want an excuse to go home. Teachers' grade books are full of zeroes behind the names of students who are technically enrolled in a course but rarely show up for class. Raids on abandoned buildings near the school typically turn up students on the lam. Administrators make regular appearances in court to discuss chronic truants and delinquent students. Jefferson's official attendance rate is "roughly 86 percent," according to one published report, but that figure accounts only for the students who stay through the first class of the day. Some teachers and administrators say the actual daily attendance is much lower.

"We have a policy that nine unexcused absences in a period are supposed to" earn a student a failing grade for the course, said veteran biology teacher Mary James Decker. "I'll probably get in hot water for saying this, but I have not heard of one time where that policy has been enforced."

She said students with excessive absences usually fail the class anyway, but some students miss frequently and still get by. These students — typically girls — will miss four or five days of school, Decker said, then return with a note from a parent asking that their absences be excused. The students make up the missed assignments and earn good grades for legitimately strong work before skipping school again for several days. The pattern continues throughout the year.

"The Wednesday before Thanksgiving, this building was empty," Decker said, "and I guarantee that half the mothers have teenage daughters at home cleaning and cooking for the holiday."

Jefferson's annualized dropout rate was 10.4 percent during the 1999–2000 school year, exactly twice the average rate for the state, according to the most recent statistics available. Just 51.9 percent of the students who enter Jefferson as ninth-graders complete the twelfth grade, a graduation rate that is among the lowest in the state and far below the state average of 81.4 percent. (Lincoln's graduation rate is 81.7 percent.) The state once required all school districts to include dropout rates in their annual report cards to the public, but after almost all of the school districts failed to meet the state's dropout standard of 3 percent or less, the General Assembly eliminated the requirement.

Administrators at Jefferson put the dropout statistics in more tangible terms during the orientation session for freshmen on the first day of the 1999–2000 school year. English teacher Rachel Davis, who joined the Gladston school district after working in another county school district, said she was "devastated when someone mentioned that out of four hundred students who start as freshmen, only about one hundred-sixty will graduate. They tried to make it positive. They said, 'Look at the person next to you and see what you can do to help them be here for graduation.' But I was just stunned. I just couldn't believe those numbers."

At both Jefferson and Lincoln McKinley high schools, too many students fail to find a place to belong and a good reason to stick around.

"When you go to high school, you get this freedom. You can go wherever you want. There are two thousand kids.

Nobody really pays attention to you," explained Tovah, a polite, soft-spoken seventeen-year-old who ended up at Transitions after being expelled from Lincoln for truancy in her freshman year. At Transitions, where she praised the staff for its hands-on attention and project-based learning, Tovah earned enough credits during regular sessions and summer school to graduate in 2000.

Before the ninth grade, she said, she was a solid B student with no history of skipping school or getting in trouble. But after several months at Lincoln, where, she said, many teachers seemed indifferent to students who couldn't understand the material and rarely assigned anything other than worksheets and questions at the end of the textbook chapters, Tovah started listening to peers who told her no one would notice if she skipped school.

To avoid alerting the office staff who called home to check on absent students, she checked in during homeroom, attended her first three classes, then left the school building about 10:15 A.M. most days. Accompanied by several friends, she hiked the nearly two-and-a-half-mile distance between Lincoln and Jefferson. Once she arrived at Jefferson, she lined up with other students who were leaving after early dismissal and hopped on a school bus that took her home. Most days, Tovah said, she and her friends would end up at "some guy's house, drinking and doing drugs." By the time the Lincoln staff caught on to Tovah's scheme, she had missed forty-five days of school and had failed math, English, and social studies.

To Dana Elmore, who served as principal of Transitions through the 1999–2000 school year, such stories are unfortunately common and provide strong evidence of the need for different types of educational settings for different kinds of students. Since 1995, Transitions has served 400 teenagers who have been expelled from six school districts in the county — the vast majority of them from the Gladston schools — because of truancy, criminal activity, or severe misbehavior, and has helped 55 percent of them graduate or stay in school. Although the statistic indicates that almost half of the students at Transitions don't succeed, Elmore believes it's an impressive record, considering that most of the teenagers have failed numerous times and in numerous ways before showing up at the alternative program.

"In reality," she said, "there is never going to be a school that serves all kids."

Yet fitting students into the high school model instead of varying the model to fit the students is exactly how secondary education operated in the United States during the last half of the twentieth century. As former Secretary of Education Richard Riley said, "The majority of our nation's high schools seem to be caught in a time warp from long ago."[1]

Only in recent years have alternative education programs such as Transitions begun to gain favor, and generally only for the most struggling or delinquent students. Despite waves of "reform" during the past four decades, most high schools still measure students' academic progress according to how many subject credits they accumulate, not how much they might have learned from each course. The typical pattern is for high schools to offer an increasingly demanding and standardized curriculum to a wider range of students through teachers who are too overwhelmed and too undertrained to know how to convey the necessary information in more than one way. To get something different, students quickly learn, you have to be academically gifted or get in trouble.

"Children come to school with diverse abilities, backgrounds, talents, and problems," David L. Angus and Jeffrey E. Mirel write in *The Failed Promise of the American High School*. "They learn different things at different rates and at different times in their development. Given that, schools emphasizing high academic standards will succeed only if educational professionals create developmentally appropriate, challenging course materials and methods for all students on every grade level. Much of the failure of modern American education lies in our avoiding the formidable task of discovering how to teach difficult subjects in ways that are both accessible to young people and yet true to the complexity and richness of the material."[2]

Instead, many communities have responded to the growing population of disaffected students by tightening security measures in schools and demanding stiffer penalties for teenagers who rebel. Very few have embraced changes that would help all students and all teachers learn how to learn. Everyone tries to blame someone else for why education doesn't live up to expectations. Parents complain about the poor quality of the nation's public schools — although they generally believe their own children's schools are adequate. High school educators blame middle school educators, who blame elementary school educators for failing to prepare students adequately, and all of them blame parents for their laxity, their genetics, and their general indifference to intellectual integrity.

In truth, the responsibility is widespread. Politicians pass laws requiring schools to meet tougher academic standards but provide neither the money nor the time for faculties to figure out how to do so. The majority of the nation's teachers in turn take only the minimum amount of required postgraduate training, including new methods of instruction, and few successfully adopt the new practices in their classrooms. In addition, parent involvement in education has remained relatively flat in the past few years.[3] Small wonder, then, that despite all we've learned in the past decade about the critically important role that high standards, quality teachers, and strong parent involvement play in academic achievement, many students — particularly those who live in urban areas — don't get any of the above.

Like the armed forces during a war, high schools concentrate on body counts — who's inside the building and who's not. Because school budgets are based on average daily attendance rates, getting students to show up is the way many schools define success and why they work so hard to deter truants.

"My assistant principals spend at least 70 percent of their day trying to get kids to come to school," Jefferson Principal Angelo Hancock says. "What we do the first time when the student is truant or absent from school, there will be a conference with the assistant principal. The second time there will be a detention. The third time we'll be calling the parent and having the parent in for a conference and the student will be placed in in-school suspension. And once they get up to five days of truancy, we file charges with the court.... Keep in mind that they [the assistant principals] also will drive up to the house and drag the kids out of bed and everything. They try to do everything. But once we file charges with the court, it's my philosophy that at this point, we're not chasing you anymore. It's going to be up to the court."

Realistically, of course, the courts don't have many options with truants. Repeaters can be charged with disobeying a court order, which earns the student a five-day trip to the juvenile detention center. But "after that, nothing happens," Hancock said. "Having been the principal at the jail [the Multi-County Juvenile Detention Center], I had a full house there with kids who were in for shooting people, kids who were in for raping people, kids who were in for doing drugs, and all that stuff. What am I going to do with a kid who's truant? Very rarely can they really do anything with a truant. The kids know it.... Finally, we'll either withdraw them if we can't get hold of them or we'll go through the expulsion procedure, and that's simply to get them off our records so the attendance rate doesn't look so bad. Because you've got maybe fifty kids that are like that. They haven't been to school. We can't get them to come to school."

All of those efforts to track down truants, however noble, mean less attention to improving instruction and, through it, raising student achievement. Some would argue that good teaching rarely happens in the chaos of a disorderly school — and certainly nationwide, parents routinely put school safety at the top of their concerns about education. Around the country, students in high-poverty schools such as Jefferson say they feel less safe than students in schools with lower concentrations of poverty.[4] But research has shown that high-quality instruction is one of the best antidotes to discipline problems and similar distractions to learning.

"Expert teachers know how to recognize children experiencing difficulties, diagnose sources of problems in their learning, and identify strengths on which to build," the National Center for Education Statistics concluded in its January 1999 publication *Teacher Quality: A Report on the Preparation and Qualifications of Public School Teachers*. "This skill is particularly important because a growing number of students with a wider range of learning needs (i.e., students whose first language is not English and students with learning differences and disabilities) are entering and staying in school."

Studies have revealed the undeniable link between effective teachers and high achievement, and the connection works particularly well for students who come from poor and disadvantaged backgrounds. Although student poverty often correlates with low achievement, test scores, and graduation rates, researchers have found that the major cause of their limited development is the weak instruction such children tend to receive throughout their school careers. In one study conducted by William L. Sanders at the Value-Added Research and Assessment Center at the University of Tennessee, low-achieving students who had the least effective teachers gained an average of fourteen percentile points on standardized tests at the end of the year, compared with an average of fifty-three percentile points for low-achieving students who had the most effective teachers.

Evidence also suggests that the impact of both weak and effective teachers can last for years. In one study conducted by the Dallas, Texas, school system, the average reading scores of fourth-graders with three highly effective teachers in a row rose from the fifty-ninth percentile to the sixty-seventh percentile by the end of the sixth grade. By contrast, average scores for a similar group of students who had three consecutive ineffective teachers fell from the sixtieth percentile to the forty-second percentile during the same period.[5]

In 1999, the Thomas B. Fordham Foundation gave the state in which Gladston resides a grade of D-plus — the national average — for the quality of its teaching force. In the foundation's "State of the State Standards" report, the state ranked near the bottom for "giving lip service to standards-based reform, but not much else." The foundation and others have found that states with well-qualified teaching staffs — determined by the state's certification procedures and whether it requires candidates to have college degrees in the fields they teach — typically rose to the top of the rankings on national standardized tests. High-performing states also tend to have for-

mal mentoring programs for new teachers and extensive professional development requirements for veteran instructors.[6]

Urban schools, in particular, have a difficult time hiring
and retaining good teachers. Schools such as Jefferson High
School typically get fewer applicants for teaching positions, and
many of those are inexperienced instructors or castoffs from
suburban school districts. Nationally, more than half the teachers in some subjects at the high school level have neither a college major nor minor in the field. Although subject knowledge
is not the only determinant of teaching quality, research suggests
that it strongly affects how well students learn. At a minimum,
subject knowledge should be the standard for hiring and placement.

In 1999, The Education Trust, a nonprofit organization in
Washington, that seeks to improve education for the poor, surveyed high-poverty schools in twenty-one states that had scored
above average on standardized math and reading tests and found
that they shared five characteristics. All were required to show
progress according to strict state and district accountability
measures. In addition, they focused on improving training for
teachers, increasing instructional time in students' weakest subjects, setting up systems to monitor students' progress, providing tutoring as needed, and helping parents become more
involved in their children's learning.

Asked whether focusing on improving instruction might
eliminate some of Jefferson High School's discipline and attendance problems, Angelo Hancock said during the 1999–2000

school year that he buys the idea in theory but isn't sold on its practical merits.

"I say that to the teachers: 'You need to make your class so darn interesting the kid doesn't want to miss it,'" he said. "I mean, that's the idea. That's very altruistic. It's fantastic. But does it work? I haven't seen anybody yet that's been able to do it. The kids that are coming every day are coming every day regardless and those that don't, don't."

Yet, Hancock and others acknowledge that more could be done to raise the level of instructional quality in the building. Assistant Principal Sheila Twomey, who was in charge of one of the Jefferson Regional Campus restructuring committees, said she learned from visiting successful schools around the country that some changes might help. Improving the connection between teachers and parents is one strategy she noted. Setting up a student advisory program is another; it would give students an adult advocate in the building and help their parents know whom to contact whenever they have questions about the curriculum or school policies. Letting teachers regularly observe some of the excellent instructors in the building also could spur improvements.

"What is it that Mary James Decker is doing? Why does she have so few discipline problems?" Twomey asked. Or Earl Kidwell, a welding teacher: "He gets problem kids but doesn't have problems with them. He takes the time to know these kids. . . . There's a lot of positive things going on here, but they're in [isolated] pockets. We have to find a way to bring them all together and get people talking to one another."

Team teaching, another instructional approach that many schools have used to good advantage, almost never happens at Jefferson, at least in part because teachers of the same subjects are grouped on the same floor. This arrangement makes it difficult for teachers from different departments to collaborate on projects, create interdisciplinary connections for students, and stay on top of developments in other fields. Some teachers have taught the same courses in the same classroom for thirty years, Twomey said.

The staid and territorial practices of the Jefferson staff extends to the school office, where until the 1999–2000 school year, two secretaries worked side by side in the same room but with a wall between their desks. Likewise, administrators rarely meet to discuss long-term strategies and schoolwide curriculum issues because they are so busy responding to the various crises that erupt throughout the day.

To Twomey, the solutions to keeping students in school will become evident when the adults in the building open their hearts, clear their minds, and commit to talking honestly about their part in making Jefferson a better place for learning.

"We mediate with kids," Twomey said, sighing, "but we don't mediate with the staff."

3

RESTRUCTURING BY COMMITTEE

From the beginning, there were competing strategies for fixing Jefferson High School. The Jefferson Regional Campus Development Committee, known informally as the Rutherford Committee because of its chairman, Michael Rutherford, president of Monument State College of Technology, examined the feasibility of creating a multipurpose educational campus in downtown Gladston, a concept that an earlier civic group had recommended. The teachers' union fixed on a plan to reshape Jefferson along the lines of four career academies: Business and marketing; communications and the arts; health, human, and public services; and engineering, industrial, and scientific technology. Meanwhile, officials with the Gladston school district were contemplating asking state government for money to help them repair Jefferson and other run-down school buildings. In 1997, when the Davidson Foundation offered the school system $10 million to fix Jefferson High School, the resulting Jefferson Regional Campus project suddenly became an amalgam of all these different proposals.

In 1991, the Gladston Professional Educators Association had recommended that the Gladston school district merge the two high schools to eliminate overlapping programs, reduce overcrowding at Lincoln, stop the competition for money and space, and improve the consistency of discipline and instruction within the two schools. But Jefferson alumni rallied in support of their alma mater, and other people expressed concern that a single high school with about 3,500 students would be too large and reduce the students' opportunities to participate in sports, school clubs, and other extracurricular activities.

Some of these arguments resurfaced on August 1, 1996, when, after meeting for more than a year and conducting four town meetings, the teachers' union submitted a plan to restructure the school system. The union previously had agreed to a cost-saving measure requiring high school teachers to teach six periods a day instead of five in return for giving teachers the right to design the curriculum and the method of delivering it to students in kindergarten through the twelfth grade. The union then organized two large committees — one at the elementary and one at the secondary level — and representatives from schools and the community spent about fourteen months studying best practices from around the country. Based on its research, as well as comments from its members and interested citizens, the teachers' union again recommended moving to a "one-school, career-oriented, mentor-strong high school," the local newspaper reported in 1996. But in addition, it proposed creating four career clusters that would be part of the high school and would let students pursue more courses linked to their vocational interests. The plan also recommended creating a freshman connections program to help ninth-graders make the transition from middle school to high school, a conversion that became more difficult when the district switched from junior high schools with grades seven through nine to middle schools with grades six through eight. Having ninth-graders at the two high schools for the first time had rattled both the teachers and the teenagers, as demonstrated by the high dropout rates, course failures, and suspension rates for freshmen. (The freshman connections project later evolved to a half-day freshman academy, which eventually became the biggest and best-implemented product of the Jefferson Regional Campus project and the main battleground for the school system's struggles with setting standards for teaching and learning.)

The union's proposal for separate career clusters borrowed heavily from one adopted by the school system in Fairfax County, Virginia, a description of which[1] was attached to a hefty report prepared by the union and submitted to the school board. According to the union's research, there were more than 300 similar career academies operating in United States high schools at the time.[2] Ted Adams, a native of Gladston who has been president of the teachers' union since 1982, said teachers had been concerned for many years that the Gladston school district had not kept up with advancements in the field of education.

"We had been hearing from elementary teachers saying, 'Nothing has been done here for a quarter of a century,'" Adams said. "So we seized that opportunity to start changing within the whole system."

Superintendent Lyndon LaGrange backed "about 80 to 85 percent" of the union's plan, including a proposal to merge the two high schools into a single, unified comprehensive high school with two campuses. He urged the board to call the combined high school Lincoln and adopt its bulldog mascot and athletic colors of red and black.

In early 1997, however, the school board unanimously rejected LaGrange's modification of the union's plan to merge the two high schools. Board members said they would add some programs at Jefferson to encourage adults to further their education and consider the downtown center a "state-of-the-art urban high school campus," but they were not willing to merge the two high schools. The board did approve the union's plan to create four career academies and a freshman academy on the Jefferson property. This entire initiative became known as the Jefferson Regional Campus project.

School Board President Gene Taylor seemed to signal the board's intent some months earlier when he publicly criticized the union's plan to expand intramural sports programs as a means of compensating students who might lose the chance to participate on interscholastic teams in a larger, merged high school.

"When's the last time you saw a good intramural program?" he asked. "Do you think a college coach goes to recruit at an intramural basketball game?"

Taylor, a graduate of and a former Jefferson teacher who had sent all twelve of his children to the school, said he would not approve any restructuring plan that involved changing Jefferson's name to Lincoln. According to the local newspaper account, he said he might support a neutral name, but not one existing school swallowing the other.

Teachers were extremely disappointed by the board's decision to keep two high schools open, Adams said. As long as the school leaders kept pretending that Gladston offered two equal schools, he said, neither would reach the necessary level of excellence. "Our contention was, 'No, that kind of defeated the whole thing'" because it would not guarantee that the two high schools would offer academic programs of similar quality, and thus, would do little to alter the enrollment reversals at Jefferson. Union representatives also wanted two of the proposed career academies to operate at the Jefferson building and two at the Lincoln site, and they were hoping for a coordinated curriculum from kindergarten through twelfth grade instead of the more haphazard focus that the school board's vote would allow to continue. Nevertheless, teachers and administrators did what they could to make the school board's plan work.

Leaders of the Gladston school district decided that the best way to proceed was to appoint people to committees and start hashing out ideas. If there's one thing that government entities do well, it's forming committees. Certainly, such study groups can serve useful purposes. They can pursue important agendas, involve diverse groups of people, designate leaders, build consensus, and delegate difficult work. But committees also can examine problems for so long that people forget their original mission, distrust the group's final decision, and end up fighting the changes they previously championed.

"Organizational change — not just in schools, but in institutions of all kinds — is riddled with paradox," Robert Evans writes in *The Human Side of School Change*. "We study it in ever greater depth, but we practice it with continuing clumsiness."[3]

The school system formed eleven different committees related to the Jefferson Regional Campus project. These included groups focusing on assessment; communications; curriculum and instruction; educational specifications, including buildings and equipment; teaching and learning; and technology. There was one for the freshman academy and one each for the four proposed career clusters: business and marketing; health, human, and public services; engineering, industrial, and scientific technology; and communications and the arts. A larger coordinating committee was supposed to guide and supervise the overall development of the Jefferson Regional Campus project. This group came to be known as the Stevens Committee because of its leader, retired Gladston Superintendent Nolan Stevens.

Finally, there was the Rutherford Committee, which was to serve in an advisory capacity, taking a more global view of the project by reviewing best practices around the nation and making connections with leaders of neighboring school districts, businesses, and higher education. Altogether, more than 130 people — mostly teachers and administrators — served on the various committees.

"They did a lot of floundering as those committees began to meet. It was like, 'Well, what are we supposed to do?'" said Jefferson Principal Angelo Hancock, a member of the coordinating, assessment, and educational specifications committees. "So the committees would meet, and for about a year those committees were really in a state of confusion."

Others take a more charitable view of the planning process, saying the volunteer members stayed busy visiting other school districts, studying building specifications, and learning about new methods of instruction, in addition to holding down their regular full-time jobs.

"You know, it wasn't as if these individuals had nothing else to do during the day," Adams explained. "Unlike industry that pulls a group of people out and says, 'This is your focus for the next six, seven months.' No, teachers were teaching all day, then coming to meetings after work."

The reorganization teams created through the union's recommendations met faithfully but without much fanfare until the spring of 1997. In June, Superintendent Lyndon LaGrange, sitting in his office at the administrative center, a decrepit, red brick former school building reconfigured as the school district's headquarters, received a telephone call from Martin Diego. The executive director of the Gladston education partnership, a local nonprofit group organized in 1989 to disperse private donations and advocate for school reform in the county, Diego had called with what he believed was great news for the school system and the community. The Davidson Foundation had just committed to spending $10 million over four years to help the Gladston school district complete the Jefferson Regional Campus project.

LaGrange said he was thrilled. But over the next few weeks, as the Davidson Foundation spelled out its goals through formal letters of intent, LaGrange and other school district leaders realized that the unexpected and unbelievably generous grant was a mixed blessing. Although it provided the means to move the restructuring project ahead, it also raised the stakes for what it must accomplish.

"The spending must be tied to clear, public, and measurable indicators that will show where and how progress is being made," wrote John Williams "Will" Davidson, president of the Davidson Foundation and a Gladston education partnership board member. "In other words, funded projects must show how they help Jefferson High School students achieve at higher levels."

Will Davidson articulated some general objectives for the project, but the grant letter provided "lots of wiggle room," as one planning document termed it. There were actually two letters spelling out the details. The first letter talked in more global terms. It spoke of the need "to develop and foster real systemic change in the educational process within Fulkerson County."

A second letter, sent four days later, identified the procedures the foundation officers expected the school district to follow. The letter said that the Davidson Foundation had intended for the $10 million grant "to support improvements — both now and in the future — of the educational *system*. Specifically, the Trustees expect changes in the students' experience at Jefferson High School (as part of the planned Jefferson Regional Campus) ensuring that all graduating students are fully prepared and qualified for work, citizenship, and continued learning."

The Davidson Foundation designated the Gladston education partnership as the "fiscal agent for the disbursement of this grant" and the group charged with helping school leaders "in the conceptual development, creation, and execution of their plans." Will Davidson made it clear that he wanted some outside oversight of the project's plans and expenditures. The partnership's staff members also were to serve on all of the committees the school system had set up to design the Jefferson Regional Campus project.

Over the next few months, the outsiders and the insiders repeatedly locked horns. The partnership's representatives thought the committees were being too deliberative, too parochial, and were spending money unwisely, such as hiring a local advertising agency to communicate developments to the public instead of involving the public in planning the project. School officials thought the partnership's representatives — Diego, in particular — were interfering in areas in which they had no direct experience and, frankly, no right. The claims and counterclaims led to a series of accusations, hurt feelings, and miscommunications over issues ranging from hiring decisions to the pace of change. At a 1997 Jefferson Regional Campus project retreat, for example, the agenda included a separate heading for "Trust Issues," including "paranoia — educators afraid they will have to streamline to be more in line with business practices" and "fear that [the Gladston education partnership] won't approve expenditures."

Designating an outside monitor for the project made school officials nervous and suspicious; it also made them defensive because it seemed as if the Davidson Foundation had entered the agreement with a high level of distrust for the people who were charged with carrying out the reforms. School officials thought the $10 million grant overshadowed the vision and stewardship of the original Jefferson Regional Campus planners, as if the grant had created the project instead of jump-started it. In addition, school officials speculated — correctly as it turned out — that if the money was earmarked primarily for changes at Jefferson High School, it would exacerbate the tensions between the two high schools, which were already vying for what Lyndon LaGrange calls "most favored nation status" within the school district.

"I was told repeatedly that the grant was strictly to be used for the enhancement of Jefferson High School and the experience students would have there," Adams said. "Lincoln was not, and if I had a dime for every time I was told it was not to be used for Lincoln, I could retire.... I don't think they realized the ramifications of the division that has been crossed in the school system. As a matter of fact, I remember at a meeting saying, 'Can't we talk to the [Davidson] foundation to explain to them what this is doing to the relationship between the two sister schools,' and I was told no. Because in my heart, I knew they never meant this to be a divisive grant."

Adams said the Davidson donation also prompted the organizers to emphasize a top-down focus that he believes was counterproductive to its efforts to involve teachers and administrators at every level of the school system. He believed that changes should start at the elementary level and flow upward, much like a tree takes in water at the roots and uses it to feed various branches. For example, the union's original recommendation was to begin the career focus in preschool so students would get a chance to explore different professions every nine weeks through the eighth grade. Then in the ninth grade, students would gain hands-on experience by rotating through each of the four career clusters, which would help them choose an area of concentration for the remaining three years of high school.

"And then it really gets muddied by this beautiful gift we get from the Davidson Foundation," Adams said. "Probably the most disappointing thing is that we weren't able to build this program from the ground up. Nothing's been done from grade eight down. And that's the feeder system."

LaGrange acknowledged that he didn't understand how all the pieces of the project should fit together and how curriculum decisions made at the high school level would affect the middle grades and all the way down the line. He said he also underestimated the degree to which the larger community would have to understand and support both the goals of reform and the sacrifices involved in changing long-standing educational practices.

"I think this community is blessed with enlightened leadership. I do not count myself among that crowd," LaGrange said. "I'm more of a traditionalist, slow to change, cynical of using kids as guinea pigs.

"…To bring about a true systemic change requires a cultural change, the change in mind-set from the student, the parent, the teacher, the school administration, the board of education, the community members, the small-business leaders, the big-business leaders, the social service agencies…. It's difficult. I'm still trying to have someone show me how to do that."

To Will Davidson, the restructuring agenda was much more straightforward than school officials made it out to be. He said he bestowed the $10 million gift because he thought it could make a difference in a single, desperate urban high school that his family had built. And if the changes were successful at Jefferson High School, leaders could share the lessons with other schools within Gladston and the rest of the country.

But the money made supporters of the other schools in the system jealous of the attention and opportunities available to the Jefferson crowd. And so a reform project that was barely off the ground started losing altitude immediately.

"Basically, the parents, faculty, and administrative people at the other schools began to say, 'Hey, they're getting all the good stuff. We don't get any. We want part of the pie, and we want it now, and if you don't get it to us, we're going to harass you,'" Davidson said. He believes these naysayers encouraged the timidity of some of the project leaders, those who "wanted to modernize what they had but not change." It was as if his family's grant had placed a neon sign around the divisions within the Gladston school system, between those who preferred to tinker with the practices they were comfortable with and those who wanted to rattle the traditional high school model down to its foundation.

The first phase of the Jefferson Regional Campus project was supposed to begin in August 1999, with the opening of the freshman academy and the business and marketing academy. By that time, however, some of the committee members had been involved in dreaming and planning for more than four years. They were weary of the changing demands of the project, the constant second-guessing from the Davidson Foundation and the Gladston education partnership, and the political snares they had to repeatedly disentangle. The pressure was on to produce.

"You start getting this message from people, 'Well, we're not going to be ready next year in business and marketing.

Would it be better if we waited another year to make sure we have it right?'" said Nolan Stevens, the project coordinator. "It was not resistance to doing it, but wanting to make sure we're going at the right pace, a fear of failure. My feeling was, we can't fear failure. We have to move forward and learn from it. If we want the public to trust us we've got to do something."

In the spring semester of the 1998–1999 school year, 328 eighth-graders had signed up for the two half-day sessions of the freshman academy, and 98 sophomores had elected to join the business academy. The Gladston community had expressed its faith in the restructuring project, but the public — particularly parents — would expect immediate results.

Yet, there was still so much to be done. Each academy needed a new or renovated building in which to operate. Transportation issues had to be resolved because students would have to be moved to and from their home high schools at various times of the day. Teachers and administrators had to be hired and trained to work in the new centers, but because of a school system hiring freeze imposed as a result of budget cutbacks, most of the "new" staff positions were actually borrowed from other schools, which created additional resentment and frustration.

The costs of the Jefferson Regional Campus project also escalated, and the competition for dollars intensified. The Gladston school district eventually secured $35 million dollars in state funding for construction, $2.5 million from state and federal sources for technology upgrades, and $2 million from the city of Gladston for infrastructure, including repairing sidewalks and roads near the renovated campus. A bond levy, which voters approved in 1999, eventually will provide $46,700,000 (matched by $149 million in state aid) for building repairs throughout the Gladston school district, including some related to the Jefferson makeover. Only $2 million of the Davidson Foundation grant can be used for building renovations and land acquisition, according to the terms specified by Will Davidson. The rest of the grant was earmarked for research and design, including training for teachers and administrators.

As the countdown to the pilot phase of the Jefferson Regional Campus project began, Nolan Stevens sometimes wondered why he'd ever come out of retirement to lead it. He had used all of his organizational strengths to put structures in place, to placate the various players, and to give every committee a set of objectives, time lines to fulfill, and information about what all of their counterparts were doing. He had tried to consider how Jefferson High School would continue to operate when all the new academies opened and how the different instructional focus at the freshman academy would affect students as they moved to and from the traditional high schools. He had helped select the directors of the new programs and engineered the fact-finding missions that included out-of-state travel for dozens of the committee members.

"The beginning, the starting, was the most complicated thing I've ever been involved in, by far," Stevens said months later. "None of us had ever done it before on this scale."

Meanwhile, life at Jefferson High School continued as usual. The changes that were swirling around the school system might well have been happening in another community for all the impact they were having on the traditions within the secondary education ranks in Gladston. At Jefferson, the first order of business was still discipline, not instructional innovation.

4

THE MAN IN CHARGE

Jefferson High School Principal Angelo Hancock could be considered a good match for a place that in recent years has had more than its share of troubled students. He used to be one himself.

By his own account, he was lucky to have made it to high school graduation. In the fourth grade, he said, he was kicked out of a local public school for misbehavior. He said the principal called his mother and told her, "'I think it would be in his educational best interest to complete his schooling in a Catholic school or private school — anywhere else.' And my mom beat the heck out of me and sent me off to Catholic school, as a matter of fact."

In the ninth grade, Hancock was scheduled to attend Jefferson High School, but his mother didn't want him to "embarrass" his brother, who worked in the system as a teacher at Lincoln High School. So instead, Hancock went to Community Catholic High School in Gladston where, he claims, he used to "get beat up all the time by the brothers [in the religious order that ran the school]. I mean, I was an ornery kid. I couldn't sit still. I was never belligerent or disrespectful or, you know, doing drugs, that kind of stuff. But I couldn't sit still. I was always into something. And there was always something happening, and it was always around me."

After graduating from college, Hancock moved to Columbus, Ohio, where he taught high school history for a year. Then he spent six years as a drummer in a jazz trio, traveling to clubs as far away as Las Vegas. After working for a time as a sales representative for a Gladston company that manufactures light poles for highway construction projects, Hancock returned to college, where he earned the first of two master's degrees. Initially, he said, he had a difficult time getting a job in area schools because of an incident during his student teaching stint at Summit Junior High School, now a middle school serving grades six through eight.

"I got an A on my student teaching, but I did have a confrontation with a student. And, of course, back in those days, this was 1967, that student just had a hard time standing up. He kind of fell all the way down to the office, and he fell into the lockers, and he fell into the principal's office," Hancock said facetiously. "He was a thug, and he had been messing around in class.... The principal didn't like the idea that I had roughed up the kid, so he told the assistant superintendent not to hire me."

When that administrator retired, Hancock found a supervisor with a more receptive ear and was offered a job teaching fifth grade in the Gladston school system. Soon afterward he moved to the old Harding High School, where he worked as coordinator of an occupational program that combined academic courses and job skills for students with behavioral disorders. From there he held a series of administrative positions, including principal of the Multi-County Juvenile Detention Center school, before getting the top job at Jefferson in 1995.

Hancock said he believed that his charge was to polish the school's tarnished image by implementing stronger discipline procedures. An early incident gave him the means to get rid of the school's worst troublemakers and, in the process, send a loud message to the Gladston community that a new man was in charge.

"On the opening day of school my second year, we had a riot," Hancock said. "It was a fight that started up in the cafeteria, and there must have been fifteen different gangs involved. The fight went from the cafeteria [on the fifth floor] all the way down through" to the first floor.

Hancock said he asked the superintendent and the school board for permission to seek felony charges against the nine worst offenders, all of whom spent time in jail. When they were released, Hancock said, he refused to let them reenroll at Jefferson.

"That made a statement to the thugs and the gang kids

that you're not going to get away with that at Jefferson anymore," he said.

It also solidified his reputation as a no-nonsense adminis-trator who would not back down from a challenge. Though he wears sharp suits and ties and keeps a fairly placid expression on his face, Hancock looks like a man who's not afraid to mix it up. He is fidgety and brusque, with a sarcastic wit that can quickly become demeaning.

One afternoon, for example, Hancock was walking through the school building when he heard the Jefferson band practicing in a classroom. He stopped in the doorway to listen. A student was singing a cappella between the instrumental pieces, but was having a difficult time hitting the required notes. Although the student was giving his best effort, his voice was flat and untrained. The band director already had sat through the rendition twice, and after each round had diplomatically suggested some modifications that the self-conscious student could make. When the music stopped the third time, the band director looked toward the doorway.

"You need me?" he asked Hancock.

"No," the principal said and smirked. "I just came in 'cause I thought the record was broke."

Several students snickered, but not the soloist. Hancock's sarcasm caused him to slump in his seat.

Although joking at an adolescent's expense might have been Hancock's boorish attempt to be "one of the guys," it sent a powerful message that picking on people was acceptable at

Jefferson. Such behavior wasn't reserved for students. Indeed, the principal's penchant for put-downs, particularly with his female colleagues, has earned him plenty of detractors within the school system.

Yet, many Jefferson students also credit Hancock with showing them tenderness and respect. "Mr. Hancock, he's really a cool principal," said Denise, a sophomore honors student. "He cares about kids. One time I had trouble with a bus driver. He wouldn't let me ride because he said I had been 'smart' with him. I told Mr. Hancock. He handled the guy. He said, 'You have no authority to refuse a student until you talk to the principal.'"

Jessica, another Jefferson sophomore with bleached blonde hair and a fondness for black leather clothes, said she appreciates the "upbeat" morning messages the principal sends on the intercom and the distinctions he makes between the troublemakers in the school and those who are intent on getting a good education. One day, she said, after Hancock caught two kids smoking on campus, discovered a fire set in the building, and ordered repairs to the windows broken in two doors, he publicly chastised those students who were making Jefferson look bad and failing to demonstrate "dignity and class." "But the next week he gave another speech and said, 'I'm so proud of you guys,'" she said.

Rick, a freshman with shaggy blond hair, saggy blue jeans, and a notoriously short attention span, said he was surprised and impressed when the principal hailed him in the hallway and called him by name. "He knows me," Rick said with obvious bewilderment and pride. "I've never been in trouble, and he knows me."

Students also praised the incentives Hancock put in place for those who earn good grades and conduct marks. Students with at least a 3.0 grade point average — essentially a B average — and no discipline problems receive a Gold card, which entitles them to go off campus for lunch, hang out in the student union during free periods, and get exempted from certain tests, pending teacher approval. Students who have a 2.8 grade point average receive a Blue card, which entitles them to visit the student union.

When the grade reports come out, students line up outside the principal's office to get their rewards. The number of scholars isn't high for a school of Jefferson's size, a problem that troubles Hancock but that he said he doesn't know how to solve. He acknowledges that many students leave Jefferson ill prepared for college and careers. Currently, he says, only about 15 percent of them attend college directly after graduation. In recent years, no Jefferson students have taken the national Advanced Placement exams that can help them earn college credit for rigorous high school courses. According to the school district's records, one-fourth of the students qualify for special education services, meaning they have identified learning disabilities or behavior disorders that impair their ability to learn.

In April 2000, when Jefferson held its annual induction ceremony for the school's chapter of the National Honor

Society, only three seniors and five juniors met the school's qualifications: a cumulative grade point average of at least 3.5 (essentially an A-minus average), teachers' recommendations attesting to the student's character and leadership qualities, and a form on which the student details his or her extracurricular activities and public service. The previous year, five Jefferson seniors and fifteen juniors qualified for the same honor.

"While accelerated courses are offered in English, math, science, and foreign language, student registration for these classes has greatly declined," the Jefferson faculty wrote in 1999 as part of the school's 1999 accreditation review from the North Central Association of Colleges and Schools. "Post-secondary opportunities are also available, yet few students participate. In the fall of 1998, in collaboration with two area institutions of higher learning, an attempt was made to accommodate students in postsecondary classes 'in house.' Low enrollment and scheduling conflicts resulted in those classes being cancelled."

Yet veteran biology teacher Mary James Decker believes she has seen some improvement in the caliber of students at Jefferson during the past few years. In the 1997–1998 school year, for example, Jefferson began offering an advanced biology class. Sixteen students signed up for it, she said. But by the 1999–2000 school year, enrollment in advanced biology had grown to forty-four students and expanded to two classes.

"We are getting better and better students," Decker said. "We have less and less criminal element…and the ones we do have are tolerated for a shorter amount of time.... I really give Mr. Hancock credit for always having a positive attitude. I think he was put here to reinstill pride and to get rid of a lot of riffraff in the building."

For all of Hancock's strengths as a disciplinarian and administrator, however, some people wonder privately if he's the right person to lead Jefferson High School in the era of reform. A reorganized high school campus made up of academies geared to students' interests, with dynamic, hands-on instruction would seem to call for a principal who has demonstrated some success as an instructional leader. Hancock acknowledged that this is not his strong suit. And though he said he believes in the goals of the Jefferson Regional Campus reforms, he also disagreed that a high school principal today can focus on both adminis-tration and instruction. A typical school day involves so many scheduling issues, discipline referrals, state and district require-ments, after-school activities, and meetings that it's tough to find time to observe classroom instruction and coach teachers to use more effective practices, he said.

"Basically I'm a manager," Hancock said. "I get here at five-thirty [in the morning], and then if there's a game or something [after school] you don't go home until ten o'clock at night, and that whole time you're doing nothing but putting out fires and handling things as they come through the door. I don't have time to do the research and actually do the education reform that has to happen. No principal does."

Actually, some do, by finding ways to use their time differently. But high school principals have more difficulty with the dual functions than their counterparts at the elementary and middle levels. The size of the typical high school compounds the challenge of steering any change initiative, and high school faculties tend to be less receptive to education reforms. Widely used instructional practices such as teaching across different subject disciplines and working with teams of colleagues, for example, have made only limited inroads at the secondary level. Some people speculate that this pattern of resistance stems from the way many high school teachers think of themselves — closer to intellectually rigorous and emotionally distant college professors than to their counterparts at the elementary level, whom they sometimes view as dispersing little more than "smiley" stickers, candy, and hugs.

Whatever a faculty's feelings, the principal plays a critical role in starting and sustaining school improvements. And research has shown that the efforts needed to ignite high levels of learning among students and teachers will not happen unless the commitment to change occurs at both personal and institutional levels.

"School principals who see themselves as instructional leaders know what constitutes quality education," Lorraine Monroe, a nationally recognized principal and author writes in the December 1999 issue of *Basic Education*, a publication of the Council for Basic Education in Washington, D.C. "They make sure that everyday in every room teachers are delivering quality instruction for all children so that excellence happens. The leaders' training, belief, dedication, and administrative practices can override all obstacles that many believe are deterrents to creating effective schools for all children.... My experience as a teacher, principal, and trainer of school leaders informs and reinforces my belief that the location of the school, the race or ethnicity of the children, the economic level, and first language of their parents have very little to do with children's academic achievement. In my schools I have seen children, whose backgrounds would drive most of us to therapy, come to school everyday and excel.... What made the difference with these students was attendance at a school where the leader was a fierce, demanding, supportive dreamer, planner, observer, and monitor of teachers."[1]

Certainly Gladston, is not the only place trying to figure out how to help administrators develop more effective leadership skills. Nationwide, foundations committed more than $350 million in the year 2000 to support principal training. The various initiatives recognize that many school leaders are woefully unprepared for the demands of a job whose responsibilities range from balancing budgets and keeping bathrooms clean to coaching new teachers and raising standardized test scores.

In some school districts, new and veteran principals are assigned mentors or consulting principals who can help them make the transition from building managers to instructional leaders. Some districts set up a formal induction process for principals similar to an apprenticeship in business. Other districts send principals to special training programs that show the administrators how to coach teachers and lead school reform initiatives. These leadership academies often have the side benefit of giving participants an informal network of principals on whom they can rely for support and advice.

"The principal is the reason the school is the way it is, and it can be toxic and pathological or it can be a profound place for promoting human learning," Roland S. Barth, the founder and former head of the Principals' Center at Harvard University, said in a recent interview with the *Los Angeles Times*.

Hancock said he initially thought he would be in charge of the reorganized Jefferson Regional Campus. Now, he says, it's better that the school district has hired a chief executive officer — Denise Bannister, a former principal, superintendent, and, most recently, president of a business school campus in a Western state. Hancock has stayed on as Jefferson's principal, a position that he considers more an operations manager than an instructional leader.

"So I run the place, and she does the restructuring," Hancock said happily.

Whether this hybrid approach will work remains to be seen. Bannister said that because there is a shortage of principals nationwide, it makes more sense to retrain the current crop in Gladston than to search for new ones. Yet, the school district conducted a broad search for an administrator to replace Lincoln Principal Clifton Rush, who left his post and accepted a newly created position with the Gladston school district at the end of the 1999–2000 school year.

As for the administrative team at Jefferson, Bannister said

she plans to get them "much more involved in the academies, much more involved in the stage of development" of the Jefferson Regional Campus project. And those who resist the reforms planned for Jefferson High School will find no quarter, she said she told administrators at recent strategy sessions. "We are going to change here," Bannister said she told her leadership team. "We are going to increase achievement. We are going to flip this self-destruction."

Hancock is trying to adjust. He said he involves the staff and students in school decision-making and shares insights with teachers about better methods of instruction. During his regular evaluations of teachers, for example, he said he hands them a sheet of questions designed to stimulate their thinking about their professional practices. He asks teachers how much time they spend on low-level intellectual functions such as giving directions, settling disputes, punishing noncompliance, and monitoring assignments in which students have to repeat factual information but not apply it. Afterward, he said, he encourages teachers to reflect on alternative instructional approaches by asking them whether and how often they let students plan lessons, use their skills in realistic settings, work together in groups, and explore issues that the teenagers themselves consider important, among other things.

"The kinds of things that are happening in all of our vocational labs is the kind of stuff that needs to happen in the regular classrooms," Hancock said. "And that's the kind of thing that I could have probably benefited from [as a student]."

But beyond encouraging them to be open to new ideas, Hancock doesn't have a clear-cut plan for helping Jefferson's teachers learn more effective instructional strategies. The union contract prevents him from firing tenured teachers who refuse to change, he said, although he has counseled some educators to move to other schools. He said he inherited a veteran staff accustomed to authoritarian principals telling them what to do. They have had few incentives to try new practices and have felt neglected by the school board and the community for more than a decade. Hancock estimates that about one-third of the faculty members are negative about the reforms proposed for Jefferson and will not alter their course for any reason.

"My faculty at this point, I think, is really apprehensive," the principal said during the first year of reform. "Change always creates anxiety. And they see things that they've been doing for thirty years that they've been told they have to change. And what that says to them is, 'I've been doing it wrong for thirty years.' Well, no, they haven't but now there is a new way and we do have to embrace that change. And there are people who have said, 'I'm not changing.'"

At the same time, there are teachers on staff at Jefferson who are open to new ideas and who want encouragement and guidance from administrators as they try to put those ideas into practice. Assisting these teachers and turning them into allies for change will be among the most important jobs in the entire Jefferson restructuring project. The successful transformation will depend greatly on the man in charge.

5

PROFESSIONAL RESPONSIBILITY

From his vantage point, an antiquated chemistry lab on the fourth floor of Jefferson High School, science teacher Patrick Alton said little had changed in his life as a result of the Jefferson Regional Campus project. Peering through the classroom window on an overcast afternoon in the spring of 2000, he could see the tops of the former office buildings that the school district converted to the business academy and freshman academy respectively, but nothing else of the educational campus and parklike setting promised during the public unveiling of the project a year and a half before. Inside the lab, the rusty metal Bunsen burners and faded wall charts containing the periodic table of elements were the same ones he used as a student at Jefferson in the early 1980s and, quite possibly, the same ones used by students when the school opened sixty-two years ago.

"It's a relic. It's like walking back into a time machine," said Alton, a good-natured young man with blond hair and wire-rimmed glasses who looks like a younger version of the late folk singer John Denver.

"It still works," he said, his arm gesturing toward the chemistry lab, which is linked by a door to a regular classroom. "I'm glad to have it. Most chemistry teachers don't have separate rooms" for labs and lectures.

In his seven years at Jefferson, Alton has learned to expect few changes in the way the high school operates. He doesn't complain. He's an easygoing teacher who has a comfortable rapport with his students, from the freshmen in his physical science classes to the sophomores and juniors who take chemistry. He is friendly with his colleagues, although he acknowledges that he doesn't know them particularly well, nor does he socialize with them outside of school.

"I talk to Mr. Tabor," the physics teacher, "in the hall between classes," Alton said, pausing to think about it. "We usually don't talk about educational issues."

It's only when you push past Alton's affable exterior that you discover how much he yearns for something more than his static professional life. He accepts, but inwardly resents, that administrators have observed his teaching only once in five years, according to the district's evaluation requirements for tenured instructors. He resents that the school's infrequent faculty meetings — "roughly once a month, if that" — primarily focus on procedural tasks, such as attendance policies, not more effective methods of instruction. Science department meetings occur just once or twice a year, he said, although the department chairman does drop by at the beginning and end of the school year to see if he needs to order any new supplies.

"Then again, I'm a professional," Alton said, reconsidering his momentary irritation. "It's my responsibility to try to improve. It's not the principal's job to get me to improve."

Asked what would help him become a better teacher, Alton described a culture that values continuous learning for adolescents and adults and instills a passion for educational excellence. That's the spirit he remembers from several of his professors in college — he can't recall having been similarly inspired by his teachers at Jefferson High School — whose dynamic instruction encouraged his choice of careers.

"The ones who did lectures, I mean, you were hanging on every word. And the ones who did labs, well, you couldn't wait to do the next lab," Alton said, remembering. "You could tell their level of interest in the subject matter was really high…. They wanted to change how students thought. They thought it [their subject matter] was important, and by the time you left the class, you thought it was important, too."

Such memories made him excited about what he heard of the emerging career academies in Gladston and about the promises of greater opportunities for professional collaborations. He was intrigued by reports of the daily group planning periods at the new freshman academy and by the collegial sharing that had filtered down to the elementary level, where his wife teaches. He was eager to try some of the instructional practice, such as block scheduling, which involves lengthening class periods to let teachers and students explore topics in greater depth. But he conceded that most of the innovations that teachers attempt at Jefferson "die on the vine" for lack of follow-through. With little chance to observe skilled colleagues who already are using recommended best practices and no opportunity to work with master teachers who can coach him, Alton conceded that he probably wouldn't vary his routine through the years.

"We really need support from other teachers and from the administration," he said. "There is just no professional comrade support [at Jefferson]. The kids come in, I close my door, and I'm there all alone. I do what I do and then the next batch comes in.

"...I had a mentor my first year [in a local middle school], but I really didn't see him much, and there wasn't much planned time during the day when we could get together. I taught my six classes, he taught his six classes, and whenever we could get together we got together, which wasn't often."

The isolation that Alton endures on an ongoing basis and the institutional neglect of his craft would make most professionals throw up their hands in despair. That these factors are so common in education, that they so greatly affect the quality of instruction in our nation's classrooms, ought to make more people outraged. Instead, in most school districts, the practices are simply accepted as a matter of course.

Although the amount of time spent in targeted and sustained professional development activities has been shown to lead to "significant improvements" in the classroom, most teachers in the United States do not participate in this kind of training. For example, only 19 percent of the nation's teachers report that they have been coached by an expert teacher through a formal relationship, yet 70 percent of those who were mentored at least once a week believe it substantially improved their instruction. A majority of the nation's teachers consider themselves well prepared for the responsibilities of their jobs in only one category — classroom management and discipline. Teachers say they are the most unprepared for duties that in recent years have been listed among the essential expectations of their profession, such as working with students who have limited English proficiency. And teachers at the high school level report receiving the least amount of support from colleagues, administrators, and parents than instructors at any other grade level.[1]

"The bottom line is that what teachers know and can do makes a lot of difference in how kids learn," says Linda Darling-Hammond, a professor of education at Stanford University and executive director of the National Commission on Teaching and America's Future. "This may seem like a no-brainer, but that's not how we've always conducted education policy in this country."[2]

Although 60 percent of the nation's teachers say they participate in common planning periods with teams of their colleagues at least once a week — and 40 percent of them believe this collaboration "improved their classroom teaching a lot"[3] — such collegial sharing is not part of the culture at Jefferson High School.

Darling-Hammond notes that teacher improvement slows and even stops after about five years unless a teacher works in a school that emphasizes continual learning, including regular opportunities to observe other teachers, critique each other's lesson plans, and work together to solve problems.[4]

The closest Patrick Alton had come to enjoying such collaboration in his eleven years in the Gladston school district was taking a college course in educational administration along with a teacher from the business academy. While he was enrolled in the course, Alton said he went to the business academy to meet with his colleague several times a week, which, he noted wryly, was more often than he ventured to the second floor of Jefferson High School during the entire school year.

Alton recalled one other time when he was able to have a lengthy dialogue about instruction with his colleagues. For several hours one afternoon in the spring semester of 2000, secondary science teachers from throughout the school district met to discuss their experiences with new textbooks adopted the previous fall. Alton said he was gratified to learn that teachers at other schools disliked the same textbook chapters that he did, kept to the same instructional pace, and emphasized similar skills. He also appreciated their insights. After listening to a Lincoln High School science teacher extol the virtues of the computer applications recommended in the textbook, Alton said he decided to reconsider using them.

"That's the first time that's ever happened to me, where we kind of talked about stuff before school started…and then we actually did get together [afterward] and talk about what worked and what didn't," he said happily.

Over the years, Alton has tried to respond to other recommended changes from the school and school district, such as limiting the time he spends lecturing and encouraging students to write more in classes other than English. He also has honored the principal's request that all teachers spend the first five minutes of each class period emphasizing basic math skills to help students improve their scores on the state's annual proficiency tests for ninth-graders. Yet Alton readily concedes that he has room for improvement.

"I know I'm not Teacher of the Year. I wouldn't pretend to be," he said. "I'm like dead center, which is okay with me." On his last evaluation he was judged to be "effective," which is below the top two categories, "outstanding" and "commendable," but above the bottom rankings, "needs improvement" and "unsatisfactory."

However, to achieve the goal of creating a world-class education hub, teachers at the Jefferson Regional Campus must be more than mediocre. They must find a way to raise the academic standards for themselves and their students, objectives they'll fail to meet by continuing to go about business as usual. For if the school's high dropout, suspension, and failure rates haven't provided enough motivation to change, its low standardized test scores might prove to be a greater catalyst.

In 1999, the Gladston school district met only five of the state's twenty-seven minimum performance measures, a ranking that placed them among the lowest in the state and in the bottom category — "academic emergency" — down from the second-to-last label — "academic watch" — earned the previous year. Districts that fall into the lowest category must submit a three-year improvement plan to the state department of education.

At the high school level, students in the state take ninth-grade proficiency exams in citizenship, math, reading, writing, and science. They must pass all five sections to graduate but can obtain an attendance certificate without it. Students take the exams beginning in the eighth grade, and they can retake sections they fail. In the eleven years since students began taking the ninth-grade proficiency tests, the scores posted by the Gladston school district have barely budged. Although scores have risen and fallen in various subjects over that time, passing percentages in every subject but science "remain level with or trail high marks posted during the early '90s," the newspaper reported.

Among Jefferson students — freshmen through seniors — who took the ninth-grade proficiency exams during the 1998–1999 school year, the average passing rates were 33 percent in writing, 39 percent in reading, 16 percent in math, 28 percent in citizenship, and 6 percent in science. Two teaching specialists now work full time tutoring the more than 600 Jefferson students who still need to pass at least one of the five exams.

If a company had turned in a similar performance, its shareholders might have stormed the annual meeting and demanded the chief executive's resignation, insisted on a radical departure from past practices, or, at the very least, sold all of their stock before losing their entire investment. In Gladston, as in most communities whose schools are in similar straits, citizens neither protested nor staged a coup. Somehow, where urban public schools are concerned, people seem to accept the conventional attitude that bad is the best they can do.

Asked for his opinion on the Gladston school district's flat test scores, Superintendent Lyndon LaGrange told the local newspaper that the district needed to refocus its staff training, using "best practices and research that works." Yet, with only two paid days a year designated for professional development, Gladston doesn't provide much in the way of assistance. In 1998, when the Gladston Professional Teachers Association complained about the poor quality of the workshops offered by the school district, officials began permitting teachers to select their own training as long as they could document their participation in an approved activity for the required number of hours. But the district does not have any mechanism in place — formal or informal — to gauge the impact of that training on instruction. In other words, did the workshop or college course lead to better teaching and learning?

Refining one's craft, whether art or acturarial science, requires many steps: staying on top of changes in the field, practicing them, integrating them with your daily habits, studying models of excellence, getting feedback from knowledgeable evaluators, then starting the process over again for each new skill. It is the rare school — rarer still, the school district — that understands the necessity of this course of action. More common is the approach taken by Jefferson High School under the direction of the Gladston school district: meeting the letter of the law but not the spirit.

Consider the implications of just one aspect of advancing a faculty's skills, the time to train. Nationwide, educators have been bombarded with new demands in the past decade, from including more students with disabilities in regular classrooms to meeting state accountability goals. However, educators haven't received commensurate time to study and rehearse different ways to accomplish those objectives. Certainly, teachers must assume some of the responsibility for adapting to the changes in education and society. But what other field expects its key players to get better without regular practice sessions, structured scrimmages, and end-of-game reviews? A more obvious question might be: How can a profession that spends so much time evaluating students' academic progress do such a poor job of evaluating itself?

"What has to change is instruction, not class sizes or teaching positions, or anything like that," says Martin Diego, executive director of the Gladston education partnership. "They're not going to get a veteran faculty to turn around and change by giving them three days of staff development, even if it's the right kind [of training]."

Teachers such as Patrick Alton hold the key. Unlike stand-out educators who are the first to try anything that might improve their skills and incompetent instructors who rarely do more than show up to monitor their classes, the vast majority of teachers fall somewhere in between. Many know they are not as effective as they could be but can't figure out how to raise the bar without ongoing assistance. They will venture outside their comfort zones if they know that someone they trust will be there to catch them when they fall. They need supervisors who not only expect more from them, but also demonstrate how to improve.

"If I had one thing to ask all the principals, it would be to be more visible" in the school, Alton said. But in the same breath, he pointed out that the administrative internship he served showed him how many other responsibilities Jefferson's leadership team must contend with on a daily basis. "I sat in with them, and it's just kids one after another in their offices," he said. They stayed busy "dealing with student discipline, the budget, the buildings and grounds, the e-mail system, the professional relationships with teachers, and the [union] contract."

It is a sad commentary on the perfunctory personnel practices of public schools that teachers such as Alton are hesitant to ask for more support from their commanders. But these frustrating experiences help explain why many educators in Gladston became so hopeful that the Jefferson Regional Campus project would shake up the status quo. Here was an initiative with enough money and resolve to alter Jefferson High School's lackluster routines — if school leaders would only recognize and seize the potential.

The teachers who served on the restructuring committees for the four career academies savored some of the professional perks that many other white-collar workers probably take for granted. In the first two years of the project, before any of the pilot career academies were opened, committee members received paid time off to travel to other communities so they could observe schools that had adopted similar programs. Mary James Decker, a biology teacher at Jefferson High School who served on the committee for the engineering and science academy, recalled being able to visit secondary schools that had developed a similar focus in Arizona, California, Florida, Missouri, and New Mexico.

"It was wonderful," she said. "It reinforced that we could do this. We got overwhelming positive feedback from those involved in the projects" that the career cluster concept could make a difference with students in urban schools. "The kids were very engaged."

To Decker, a twenty-three-year teaching veteran, being able to see best practices in action was more helpful than just about any other professional training she can remember. "I learned more about education in that one year than I had since I graduated from college. For our academies to be successful, we're going to have to build on staff development because if you haven't had an opportunity to see that in action, you're not going to be able to do it." In the past, she said, teachers had to "beg, borrow, and steal" to go to a one-day workshop in Hillsborough (about sixty miles away) and then had to find a substitute teacher to fill in while they were gone.

Earl Kidwell, who has taught welding at Jefferson since 1980 and who graduated from the school in 1962, said he was invited to make two of the out-of-town trips even though he didn't have an official role on the engineering and science committee. Kidwell said committee chairwoman Regina Crews wisely encouraged other teachers whose jobs would be affected by the career academy to join the fact-finding missions.

"She realized the people who are doing this are going to have to sell it," he said. "I must admit when they got started, I said, 'This is a joke.' But once I got to go on some of those trips, I really changed my mind. I'm really excited about it."

Yet, Kidwell and most others on Jefferson's staff have not been involved in the planning on an ongoing basis. They don't know how the new academies will change what they currently do and where they will fit in under the reorganization scheme. They hear bits and pieces about the campus redevelopment, both rumors and official announcements, news that causes their spirits to alternately sink and soar.

Earl Kidwell, Patrick Alton, and Mary James Decker all hope they will find appropriate positions at the engineering and science academy. They want to be part of something that will restore Jefferson High School to its former grandeur and make their jobs more meaningful. But their enthusiasm is tempered by their concern for how their professional lives might change.

Decker, for one, said she's not convinced that all the recommended innovations will work at Jefferson. For example, she
considered it "way too babyish" for high school students to participate on teams where they could collaborate with their peers
and work with the same group of teachers on a variety of related projects. And although she strongly believed that teachers
need to "make our education more real" for students through
hands-on exploration of topics, she also feared that some of the
structure and rigor of subjects might get lost if the faculty
strayed too far from traditional forms of instruction.

The Jefferson Regional Campus project represents "a huge
change for me as a teacher," Decker said. "It's very nontradi-
tional. I wonder a lot about it. Do I have what it takes? Am I
advanced enough in my skills and technology to provide what's
needed? I have some anxiety."

Such concerns are understandable. Change is difficult. It
makes people apprehensive and insecure, if for no other reason
than it implies they might not have been as effective as they
thought. To many, change symbolizes a failure of tradition
instead of an advancement of knowledge. But understanding
that some teachers feel threatened by change is the first step in
showing them how to move to a safer level, either by improving
their skills or asking them to leave. Until they identify and insist
on stronger practices, schools will continue to subject students
to instructors who can impair their ability or their motivation to
learn. Rusty Bunsen burners might make teaching more diffi-

cult, but rusty minds can make it impossible.

6

INSTRUCTION THROUGH INTIMIDATION

The Jefferson High School teacher stood outside his classroom, greeting students as they entered. He smiled pleasantly, but his gaze was stern. When the bell rang, he closed the door and moved inside, beginning the class as a coach might conduct a pregame locker room meeting.

"Okay, folks, listen up," he bellowed. "I have your homework up here. You'll have to come up and get it. We have a lot to do. I need to get attendance first."

In a short, clipped tone, the teacher began reading the roster, glancing up to spot students as he called their names, often getting no response because many students were absent.

"What's wrong with you?" he hollered at one student, a sullen boy who was dressed in an overcoat and slumped in a desk several sizes too small for his body. "You don't sit here. Get over there."

The teacher then turned to a female student in another row and changed his tone. "We don't do candy in here," he said respectfully. "Let's put that away, please."

Next, he divided the class into teams to play a takeoff of the popular television game show *Jeopardy*, which he had designed to prepare students for a test the next day. After announcing the various categories, the teacher reviewed the rules of the game, then took his place behind an overhead projector, which magnified the categories on a screen hanging over the chalkboard. It was a rudimentary version of the real *Jeopardy's* electronic game board, but technology is not readily available within the classrooms of Jefferson.

"A lot of you get caught up in wanting to win," he said, "but the object is that you understand this stuff."

His booming voice and intimidating style seemed to shout "order!" Students' desks were organized into symmetrical rows facing the chalkboard where the teacher had posted his grading scale for their class notebooks: Content — ten, Organization — ten, Neatness — ten, Accuracy — ten. Apparently, fully forty points of a student's grade for the term would be measured not by mastery of skills but management of information.

The teenage students sported oversized Tommy Hilfiger sweatshirts, heavy gold necklaces, and baggy jeans barely hanging on their hips. They seemed grouped by ability, or at least by their attention spans, with two teams of students alternately socializing, snoozing, and slouching in their desks and two other teams actively competing to win.

Only a few students were consistently accurate, including one boy, known in this class and others for being highly intelligent; he correctly answered all but one of the questions posed to his team. The teacher repeatedly praised the boy and occasionally called on him to give answers when other teams were stumped. At the same time, the teacher routinely mocked slower students, taunting them when they gave the wrong response or mispronounced words.

"Please pick a category so you can get *at least one* right," he said to a boy who had been quiet during most of the class, perhaps hoping to go unnoticed.

"Oh, uh, [blank] for one hundred," the student said, smiling nervously.

"I *think* you can get this one right," his teacher replied sarcastically. "At least I hope you can."

With that, the teacher posed the next question. The student stuttered and mumbled something before saying that he didn't know the answer.

"What? Come on," the teacher said, laughing derisively, and several students joined in. "What category did you pick?"

The boy answered with the name of the category, then realized it also was the answer to the question. He smiled, partly embarrassed by the negative attention, but also a little proud of himself for having recognized the right response.

With a dramatic roll of the eyes and an exaggerated sigh, the teacher said to the scorekeeper, "All right. *Finally*. Give Team

Three one hundred points."

"Is that going to be on the test?" asked a small and serious male student.

"Yes. That's why I told you to listen to the questions and don't worry about the game," the teacher said with exasperation.

"Oh," the student responded, shrinking into his desk.

The mixed messages this teacher was sending obviously confused the boy. He had told the students at the outset that the goal of the game was to understand the course material, not to win, but his competitive nature and penchant for being the center of the learning process had given students the opposite impression. Students understood that what mattered most to their teacher was getting the right answers *in order to win.*

The bell rang, signaling the end of the period. The seventeen students who had shown up for class that day bounded out of the room, at least a dozen of them temporarily saved from their teacher's barbs.

In retrospect, playing a game to prepare his students for an upcoming test was a conceptually sound but poorly implemented idea. Games can be a good way to get students involved in learning, often making seemingly irrelevant or unimportant topics fun and interesting. However, when competition takes precedence over collaborative learning, and when a teacher colludes with quicker students to make other students feel inferior, the spirit and the potential benefit of the game are lost. Although bright students sometimes enjoy competitions that enable them to show what they know, there weren't many advanced students in his class that day. Average students who do not enjoy competitive activities usually can learn to endure them and still perform well. But the playing field is different for slower and more self-conscious students who can become so immobilized by academic competition that they shut down. Shaming and humiliation tactics might get some teenagers to pay attention for the short term, but like spanking or hazing such practices teach youngsters that "belonging" requires a heavy price.

In a school where the faculty was less isolated than at Jefferson, teachers such as this one might benefit from having peers and supervisors watch their instruction and offer constructive feedback. ("Great idea for the game, but let's look at how you could improve the process.") Without that kind of assistance, however, he and his colleagues might never know why they fail to motivate some students and how they might change their practices to help more succeed. It's not surprising that in a school where discipline is more highly prized than imaginative instruction, discussions about good techniques are rare.

"The life force of teaching practice is thinking and wondering," Simon Hole and Grace Hall McEntee write in an article in *Educational Leadership*. "We carry home those moments of the day that touch us, and we question decisions made. During these times of reflection, we realize when something needs to change…. We need to consider the underlying structures within the school that may be a part of the event and examine deeply held values."[1]

Pitting students against each other, signaling that you have different expectations for what they can accomplish, is one way to keep them in line. The successful students do most of the work and the others try to stay invisible. But such practices serve to reinforce the misperception that only some students can learn. Unfortunately, at Jefferson and many other urban high schools, struggling students typically fulfill that prospect.

7

A COMFORTABLE PLACE TO LEARN

Leslie Newton expects her students to come to class and *try* to learn. And most of them do. Her students' attendance rates are consistently high, and only one persistently sleeps through her geometry class. Although these might not seem like impressive statistics to an outsider, they compare quite favorably with many of Newton's colleagues at Jefferson High School.

It couldn't be ambience that encourages students to show up for Newton's classes. Her room includes the same outdated furniture and equipment crowded into a small space, desks are arranged in uniform rows with narrow aisles, and the lighting seems perpetually dim. And, as with most of the school's classes, there's order if not always inspiration — the teacher talks and the students sit quietly and listen.

Newton's preferred instructional method follows traditional lines. She closes the door and starts class as soon as the school bell rings, lecturing loudly from the front of the room. But her adherence to some of the negative and more rigid characteristics of what critics call the "drill and kill" method of teaching stops there. One difference is that Newton shows students that she cares about them as individuals, not simply whether they understand polygons and the Pythagorean theorem. When she asks one student why he doesn't have his textbook open, and he tells her his locker is in a separate building, she doesn't automatically assume that he's being forgetful or defiant.

"I don't have time to go get my stuff" and make it to class on schedule, he explains.

Briefly commiserating with the student about the many logistical complications of the large high school complex, Newton lets him borrow her textbook and suggests that he ask his counselor for a locker in the main school building.

"I'm sure he'll give you one," she assures him, then moves on with her lesson.

The gesture is just one reason why students in Newton's math classes behave. They respect rather than fear her. Although her voice is loud and commanding, her face reveals compassion, and her sweaters and denim slacks suggest a casualness that doesn't end with her wardrobe. In a word, she's approachable. Firm but fair, Newton evenly distributes her disciplinary comments so neither the slow nor the inattentive students get more attention — positive or negative — than their brighter, better-behaved peers. Privately, Newton explains that the twenty-six ninth- through twelfth-grade students in her Geometry II class range from freshmen taking honors courses "to those who shouldn't even be in here." Nevertheless, Newton tries to work with all of them and build from what each student knows.

"I don't get it," a student says during one class period, interrupting Newton's explanation of triangular measurements.

The student's comment prompts Newton to visually assess the room, and she notices the confused faces of several other students.

"I'm going to try to explain and try to make it less confusing," she calmly assures him. "It really makes a lot of sense."

She animatedly draws geometric figures and formulas on the chalkboard and tries to build comprehension through a series of examples. Most of the students busily take notes, and many begin to nod in understanding. Then, to make sure the explanation got through, Newton asks for a handful of volunteers to solve additional problems on the chalkboard and explain the process to their classmates.

Unfortunately, Newton doesn't regularly show students how geometry relates to the real world. Her class mostly consists of exercises that teach students how to memorize theorems and use them to solve problems, with little application. After about forty minutes of lecturing and showing students how to tackle math problems, Newton wraps up with a few minutes to spare.

"Does everybody understand what we covered today?" she

asks. "I'm looking at a possible quiz on Tuesday."

Newton reviews what students can expect during the rest of the semester, then asks them to work quietly on their homework or study for the upcoming quiz.

"Hey, guys, you're supposed to be working," she calls to a group of students whose conversation grows too loud, and they immediately become quiet.

After talking with a few students who approach her for help, Newton casually walks around the classroom chatting with several students and helping others solve equations. When she tries to get a student to comply with the school dress code, her manner is unthreatening.

"Tony, is that a comb in your hair?" she asks a boy who has wedged a rakish comb into his cropped Afro. He smiles, nods, and removes it without protest, and Newton issues a sincere "Thank you." There is no accusation and no encouragement of other students to poke fun at Tony.

The combination of structure and steadiness works in Newton's classes because many of her students find little evidence of either quality in their homes. Newton has developed an almost innate understanding of her students' needs and temperaments, and they sense it. When teachers are competent, caring, and comfortable with students, they command respect. When teachers don't project those traits, teenagers either take charge or check out.

In its 1997 survey of American high school students, the nonpartisan group Public Agenda found that students respond very favorably to a teacher's initiative and compassion. More than two-thirds (69 percent) of teenagers said they learn "a lot more" from teachers who treat them with respect and provide individual help. Nearly equal percentages said they respond well to teachers who explain lessons carefully, care about them personally, and challenge them to do better. The survey further found that "youngsters make clear yet subtle distinctions between 'good' and 'bad' teachers. Their expectations of an ideal teacher are very high: they want interesting, engaging teachers who care about them personally and have a special knack for getting them to do their best. But they also voice respect for teachers who are demanding and consistent, whether or not they qualify as 'entertainers of the year'....If teenagers have a clear, and surprisingly flexible, notion of what makes a good teacher, they also have very distinct ideas about what makes a teacher, in their words, 'bad.' As suggested earlier, being strict or demanding is not what teens resent most. Instead, youngsters complain about pointless and toothless threats, meaningless or tedious assignments, and perhaps worst of all from their perspective, the message that, 'You can't learn, and you don't matter.'"[1]

Leslie Newton's classroom is a comfortable place to learn. Students show up because they feel encouraged — if not inspired — to do their best. They recognize that if they attend class and try, Newton will do everything she can to help them succeed. But like most of her colleagues at Jefferson High School, Newton doesn't have all the tools necessary to be a great teacher. Without regular observations, assessments, and coaching from experienced peers and mentors, she cannot engage in the reflective practice that research shows helps teachers grow on the job. In the absence of instructional leadership, teachers might improve, but no one monitors whether they do. Perhaps most importantly, no one establishes the expectation that they should.

PART II

The Remodeling Project

8

THE FIRST LEVEL OF REFORM

On a Saturday morning in December 1999, Scott Peterson sat in a conference room at the freshman academy reflecting on the first semester. Halfway through the school year, the dean of students wondered what had happened since the faculty members convened the previous summer to profess their dedication to the oft-stated philosophy that "no student would be left behind." Peterson had thought they would be closer to realizing that goal by now, yet too many kids were still failing, too many had disengaged from their schoolwork, and too many just seemed lost. There were signs of progress; Henderson could see that, from the high-quality student work samples decorating the hallways to the declining number of discipline referrals to the office. But he worried that the successes were still too sporadic and that they might be undercut by the refusal of some teachers to honor their commitment to change.

"In the summer there was a lot of energy there with people, and I thought, 'Man, this is, like, thirty people who really think highly of kids and want to do really great things with kids,'" he said. "And I [thought]...'Wow, what an opportunity.'"

Peterson's voice trailed off. A student who was cleaning tables in the science lab came in and reported that he had finished his task. Peterson had promised to buy the boy lunch before driving him home. This particular student had come so far, Peterson explained out of earshot. Because of his troubled home life, he had spent a lot of time living on the streets. He had neglected his schoolwork, skipped class, and directed his anger at teachers and classmates. After many interventions, Peterson had bonded with the boy, going so far as to attend therapy sessions with him and getting him to agree to check in every morning so the dean would know he wasn't truant. It seemed like a lot of trouble for one kid, but Peterson sloughed it off. It's part of his job, he said. He wouldn't stop trying to save another teenager just because the assignment proved challenging.

Peterson doesn't have to work on Saturdays, but he usually does. Most weekends he organizes several hours of pickup basketball for a group of students whom he believes would benefit from the exercise and structured activity. Afterward, he catches up on paperwork, often while one or two other students perform odd jobs, such as cleaning graffiti from the classroom furniture, wiping fingerprints and scuff marks from the walls and stairwells and, when Peterson runs out of school projects, painting the fence at his home. Some of the students who participate in these informal Saturday sessions are poor and want to earn spending money, which Peterson pays out of his own pocket. Some students come from homes without any solid family structure, living with relatives because their parents are in prison or addicted to drugs and alcohol, or sleeping at a friend's house to avoid the abuse or neglect they know awaits them at home. Others must log their community service hours as prescribed by the freshman academy curriculum, or worse, by the Fulkerson County Juvenile Court. Most of these kids attach themselves to Henderson because they are desperate for a supportive father figure, and he readily accepts the surrogate role. Whatever their reason for being there, the students' presence on a Saturday serves as a reminder that the high school years certainly aren't what they used to be.

The only faculty member at the school on this particular weekend, he admits to being frustrated that many of the other educators don't spend more time after school working with struggling students. Peterson and his wife have no children of their own, so she supports his commitment to serve students whenever and however he sees fit. Two fellow freshman academy teachers usually participate in his Saturday basketball games, and Peterson understands that some teachers have young children at home or coach school athletic teams after school. But he also knows that he can't be the only safety net for teenagers in need.

"I think the school environment is where our last hope is

of saving this generation of kids," Peterson says, throwing his hands up dramatically, then dropping them as he momentarily tires of his lonely crusade. "If you look at all of the other institutions of society, they've all pretty much checked out on this group of kids…and they've all pretty much bailed out from the inner city, and the only place that's still here is the school, because we have to. We don't get a choice."

On one level, Peterson is right. Public schools do have to take whoever walks in the front door and try to steer them in the right direction. But the difficulty of the task has worn down so many educators that they have run out of energy and ideas. As a result, many students do not receive instruction that is both rigorous and pertinent to their lives. Two-thirds of American teenagers acknowledge that they could do much better in school if they tried, but they overwhelmingly identify the classroom teacher as the key to tapping their full potential. "Teachers, from the teenager's point of view, are the most important variable in whether they learn or not," the nonpartisan research group Public Agenda reported in 1997. "When students are pressed to name *the one change* that would be most important in helping them learn more, 'having good teachers' easily tops the list.'….It is also true, however, that as a group, public school teachers do not earn rave reviews from their students." Only 46 percent of students in public schools say their teachers know their subjects well, 30 percent believe their teachers care about them personally, and 33 percent say their teachers challenge them to do better.[1]

Although today's high school students overall are taking

more mathematics, English, and science classes than at any point in the last quarter century, they often do not take consistently challenging courses that will prepare them well for college and careers. For example, less than one-third of United States students from low-income families are enrolled in the college-preparatory track in high school, compared with two-thirds of students from families in the upper-income range. And research shows that the high school curriculum a student follows has more to do with a student's success in college than any other factor.[2]

"One of the biggest problems is that the folks who are most important in the teaching and learning equation — high school teachers and students — often do not know about the differences between what higher education demands, in terms of both courses and test content, and what K–12 requires for a diploma," contends The Education Trust, a national nonprofit group that advocates for greater equity for poor students. "By requiring all students to complete rigorous college preparatory classes instead of just any old class that fills an open slot, schools can stretch student minds — and stretch their results."[3]

Kati Haycock, director of The Education Trust, acknowledges that the assignment for urban schools is complex. "We know that it will be much harder for many schools and districts serving concentrations of poor and minority children to get their students to high-level standards than for schools serving students with every advantage. In many of the former schools, the curriculum has slipped to very low levels, instructional materials are insufficient and out of date, and teachers are more likely to be undereducated in the subjects they are teaching. Yet this challenge must strengthen our resolve, not sap our courage. We know that these students can achieve these high standards. Our job as a nation is to make sure they get an education calibrated to achieve that end."[4]

The freshman academy was designed to fill many of those gaps. It sprang from the belief that urban students would rise to the level of expectations set for them and that, with the right kind of supports, they could compete with the best of their peers. The organizers positioned this promising new program precisely at the point where history had shown that teenagers tended to fall off course. Beginning in the ninth grade, students decide either that school serves a useful purpose or it doesn't. Too old to follow rules just because adults say they should but too young to avoid the state's compulsory education laws, they search for meaning among the mixed signals society sends.

In the Gladston school district, ninth-graders made up almost half the suspensions in the district through the 1997–1998 school year. In addition to these discipline problems, ninth-graders in Gladston had poor attendance rates, repeated tardiness, and high levels of failures in both high school courses and standardized tests, according to a report of the Jefferson Regional Campus project.

The Gladston schools don't exist as an island. Problems with freshmen plague many American high schools. One reason, according to education experts, is the lack of well-developed transition programs from the middle grades to high school. Students experience such a wide range of personal changes during adolescence that the culture shock of moving to larger and more impersonal secondary schools coupled with the greater expectations for independence and maturity compound their insecurities. Many students can't immediately make the intellectual and emotional leaps that high schools expect. Adolescents aren't widgets. They come in all shapes and sizes, and their emotional, physical, and mental development doesn't always keep pace with their chronological advancement.

Judy Hummel, the Center for Leadership in School Reform consultant who works with the freshman academy staff, said she hears the same comment in schools all over the country: "What can we do to help freshmen? We're killing them." No matter where she's coaching, Hummel said, "I hear this question asked over and over again. Our high schools are mean-spirited places that are only punitive for most students."

As envisioned, the freshman academy would be "a learning center" set up to "meet the individual student's needs" and "challenge each student to achieve excellence." Instead of moving to different teachers and different subjects every fifty minutes — the traditional compartmentalized high school schedule — freshman academy students would stay with the same team of math, science, English, social studies, consumer science, and technology teachers throughout the year. This instructional model, the recommended approach for middle schools, was designed to help teachers and students work in concert instead of treating each subject as a discreet field that has no relation to the others. By working together to show students the connections among related subjects, each team of teachers would emulate the workplace where people with various specialties often must join forces to solve problems on the job. At the same time, the ninth-graders would gain experience applying "knowledge from one discipline to another," a brochure about the freshman academy claimed. Each team would "vary the use of time in the classrooms depending on what's needed for students to accomplish their work."

In addition, the freshman academy was supposed to work in tandem with the two high schools in Gladston, although its organizers clearly hoped their accomplishments would inspire the two stalwarts to change their practices, too. During its pilot phase, the 1999–2000 school year, the freshman academy was slated to accept about one-third of the ninth-graders from Jefferson and Lincoln high schools and eventually serve all the freshmen in the Gladston school system. Students would attend the freshman academy for half a day — a morning or an afternoon session — then spend the rest of the time at their chosen high schools. To make sure the program attracted a wide range of students, the freshman academy offered them the possibility of earning an extra academic credit for the year because of an expanded emphasis on career exploration and technology applications.

The Jefferson Regional Campus plan also called for a new building to house the freshman academy, which would include

all the accoutrements of a regular high school, minus the cafeteria and athletic facilities. However, as with many other parts of
the restructuring plan, the time line for program development
didn't coincide with the district's schedule for physical construction, so a former medical office building two blocks from
Jefferson High School was converted into the freshman academy in the summer of 1999. The renovated building was clean,
well lighted, and newly painted. It was stocked with computers
in every classroom, a separate technology lab, and small offices
for each team of teachers. But the building lacked a library, a
lobby, a cafeteria, permanent classrooms for all of the teachers,
and an adequate number of lockers for students' backpacks and
coats — limitations that would become recurring sore spots for
the participants in the first year.

Janey Lewis, a respected former English teacher at Lincoln
High School and coordinator of the Gladston school system's
program for academically gifted students, was chosen to be the
freshman academy's program leader, another name for principal.
Lewis also had served as chairwoman of the restructuring committee that had spent about eighteen months developing the
freshman academy model. For her main assistant, Lewis tapped
Scott Peterson, a veteran social studies teacher at Gladston's
Hoover Middle School, who had extensive experience with team
teaching and a strong reputation among parents and students as
an educator who would go to any lengths to help kids succeed.

Lewis and other members of the restructuring committee
tried to improve the district's standard hiring practices by

increasing the number of requirements for the freshman academy's teachers and the number of people who would evaluate
them. So in addition to clearly defining their qualifications and
duties, they assembled an interview panel that included curriculum specialists from the district and people who had served on
the Jefferson Regional Campus committees. They asked all job
candidates to bring resumes, copies of their state teaching certi-
fications, three references, and, if they chose to, portfolios that
included samples of their assignments and their students' classroom work.

The staff they subsequently hired ranged from veterans to
first-year instructors. Five faculty members came from outside
the Gladston school district. Those chosen from within the district included teachers who had enjoyed celebrated careers at
either the high school or middle school level. Some were considered knowledgeable in their subject areas but had chafed
under what they considered controlling administrative practices
and limited professional growth opportunities at both Jefferson
and Lincoln high schools.

Many of these men and women were strangers to each
other. Although some knew of each other by reputation, they
had never worked together. To be successful, however, they
would have to quickly forge relationships and develop compati-
ble teaching styles so they could fulfill the academy's mission of
showing students how to work cooperatively to achieve greater
academic gains. And in less than two months, they were expected to move from handshakes to handholding.

In one way or another all of these teachers had agreed that they wanted to team with other professionals and design exciting new projects to make learning matter to students. As it turned out, some were better at selling themselves than performing the job for which they had auditioned. In a few cases teachers had applied for the freshman academy slots to escape problems in their previous positions. In other instances, teachers truly wanted to be part of the program but had not counted on having to change their practices and temperaments as much as the designers expected. Although they said they believed in collaboration, project-based learning, interdisciplinary teaching, and all of the other innovative instructional approaches the freshman academy organizers wanted the faculty to use routinely and well, their promises sometimes proved to be hollow.

Hiring a good staff for the freshman academy faculty demonstrates the difficulty of trying to equate job interviews with job performance. In education, supervisors can check references and ask questions to determine a candidate's personality and professional beliefs. They can look for subjective signs that the teacher will "fit" with the school's culture. Yet, more often that not, they must make judgments based on unrevealing paper credentials: Can she teach math? Will he be able to coach the track team after school? Is she certified by the state to teach grades five through eight or grades seven through twelve, and which configuration will help me cover two sections of middle school science and three classes of high school English?

Unlike corporate America, schools don't clearly articulate

the outcomes they expect of the professionals whom they hire. Teachers don't have sales quotas, regular deadlines, and customer service requirements to meet. In the recent push for greater school accountability, states have begun asking teachers to help boost students' standardized test scores to defined levels, but it's the rare school or school district that bases its performance evaluations on a teacher's ability to ensure that all students attain subject mastery. For the most part, the professional expectations focus on the various roles that teachers fill in a school: instructor, coach, moderator, hall monitor, and informal guidance counselor.

Lewis recalled that when she accepted her first teaching job more than twenty years ago, she received no real direction or advice from her supervisors or colleagues. "The principal handed me the textbook, told me I would be teaching eighth-grade English, and said, 'By the way, I need you to coach cheerleading, too.'"

Besides the traditional limitations of school hiring procedures, the freshman academy coordinators had another restriction that kept them from ensuring that every position was filled with the very best person for the job: They were required to give priority to teachers from within the Gladston school district. Because the school district had imposed a freeze on new hires, the total number of teachers throughout the system couldn't exceed 1,000. The freshman academy and business academy would have to "steal" positions from other Gladston school district. For example, when the freshman academy selected twenty-eight teachers from the Gladston district, the principals of the schools where they had previously worked could not replace them.

The policy made sense logically; student enrollment wasn't increasing, merely shifting, so the teachers would be expected to change places, too. But it irked administrators whose staffs were being raided, and it irritated many teachers who felt the crunch of additional course loads and leadership responsibilities, not to mention the loss of trusted colleagues. At one districtwide faculty meeting, Superintendent Lyndon LaGrange made repeated references to the high expectations the district had for the freshman academy and reiterated how everyone would be watching and waiting for signs of progress. He emphasized the smaller student–teacher ratio, the additional team planning periods, and the greater financial resources available to the freshman academy staff. His comments made some staff members jealous and resentful of the special attention bestowed on the staff. When some freshman academy teachers later visited Jefferson and Lincoln high schools, they got cool receptions from their former colleagues. Other educators became disgruntled when they discovered that they had been passed over for positions at the freshman academy and the business academy — there were three applicants for every available job. All of these factors combined to spread more hard feelings than congratulatory handshakes. As a result, the two academies, which represented the first tangible changes within the Jefferson Regional Campus, opened in an atmosphere that blended optimism and excitement with anger and alienation.

"I didn't get to replace thirteen teachers and had to do my master schedule over three or four times, and I'm pulling my hair out," Angelo Hancock, principal of Jefferson High School, explained during the 1999–2000 school year, adding that administrators at some of the elementary and middle schools hurt by the transfers also became disgruntled. "So it gave the [Jefferson Regional] campus itself somewhat of a bad image, which we're kind of still fighting."

For Lewis and Peterson, solving the personnel puzzle was no easier. Besides having to deal with the resentment of people whom they had overlooked or inadvertently overburdened, they had to quickly build camaraderie among faculty members who hailed from different schools with varying cultures and traditions. The freshman academy staff had uneven levels of experience and inconsistent instructional strengths. Most would be trying out new methods of teaching and testing while they were learning these processes themselves, all the while under the lens of inspection from people inside and outside the school system. They had to design more effective lessons, define distinctive discipline practices, and steer everything toward the state's academic standards and the all-important state proficiency exams.

To help them, Lewis and Peterson used part of the Davidson Foundation grant to hire consultants from the Center for Leadership in School Reform, a Louisville, Kentucky, firm that specializes in helping educators navigate the rough terrain of educational change. Led by Phillip C. Schlechty, a nationally recognized creator of professional development for educators and author of *Schools for the 21st Century*, the organization's trainers agreed to help Lewis and Peterson design summer sessions for the freshman academy faculty and coach the staff throughout the school year. Lewis and Peterson knew that, more than anything else, the success of the program would depend on the staff's ability to infuse the school with high-quality instruction that motivated teenagers to achieve and strong personal relationships that made them want to show up for class.

The plans were ambitious, the schedule was tight, and the high expectations permeated every activity that was part of the preparation for the freshman academy. Although Lewis had visited other ninth-grade centers around the country and had studied the experiences of schools that had initiated substantive reforms, she knew the first year would be full of frustrations and surprises. No amount of planning could anticipate all the obstacles that people would put in place when they realized how difficult it is to change long-standing habits.

"You know when you get in the throes of all this that there are going to be people who are disgruntled, who aren't happy, and it's harder than they thought it was going to be," Lewis said midway through the school year. "I'd say at this point, we're at the first level of reform. We know what the target is. We know some of the ways to get there.... But it's hard to stay there on a daily basis."

9

A NEW KIND OF TEACHING

The audience laughed from the first moments of watching the televised episode of *I Love Lucy*. In the recorded version, actors Lucille Ball and Vivian Vance, portraying their television characters Lucy Ricardo and Ethel Mertz, were working together in a candy factory. After briefly showing them how to package chocolate pieces streaming by on a conveyer belt, the supervisor reminded them that this was their last chance to succeed — they already had failed to perform four other jobs in the factory.

"If one piece of candy gets past you," the supervisor admonished them, "you're fired!"

She left, and Lucy and Ethel started working on their own. At first, the task seemed easy. All they had to do was pluck the small chocolates off the conveyor belt, wrap them in tissue paper, and stuff them into boxes. But as the line speed increased, the assignment became more difficult, and the two women quickly fell behind. Desperate to keep the candy from reaching the end of the line, they tried eating some of the extra pieces, stuffing others into their uniform pockets, and mashing more into the boxes than they were designed to hold.

Although the characters' antics were absurd and hilarious, they also sent a message that reached beyond the confines of a comedy show. For as the lights went on in the meeting room, and the television screen grew dark, the three dozen educators who had been watching the videotape couldn't stop talking about the episode's connections to high school.

"It's just like the education system," one teacher blurted out. "They just put you out there without any training and say, 'Go to work.'"

Another educator said she saw similarities in how teachers typically march through the textbook or designated curriculum without determining how much the students already knew about the subject or needed to know.

"Everything is thrown at kids, and they have no explanation for why or how," one teacher commented. "There should be some intervention. Why were they failing?"

"The person in charge needed to stand there and watch and see how they were learning," observed a colleague.

"They didn't expect them to succeed anyway," another said. "It was their last stop before getting fired. There was no expectation for success."

Next, they brainstormed ways they might have been able to improve the factory situation. One teacher suggested letting the workers "control the speed until they got it right." One focused on the need to hire more employees to keep up with the demands of the job. Another suggested creating an atmosphere in which the workers would feel safe enough to report snags in the production process and work together to solve problems. The question was, Could they make similar changes in their own classrooms? And could they do so without repeating the mistakes made in the candy factory episode?

The conversations continued a short time before Judy Hummel, the workshop leader from the Center for Leadership in School Reform, interrupted to remind them of the point of the exercise. "It's very hard when you're in the heat of battle to keep in sight what you're supposed to be doing," said Hummel, a former superintendent and director of a professional development center. In other words, the speed and complexity of change can cause people to derail the train before it ever reaches its destination.

Hummel could have been speaking to employees of a manufacturing company whose market share was being challenged by foreign competitors. She might have been addressing leaders of a political party whose formerly loyal voters had started switching to the other side. That she was addressing teachers was significant only in that they were new to the process of responding to present and future trends in their profession. Yet all of these groups share a common goal: learning to reform their ineffective practices before their traditions render them obsolete.

"There comes a time in the cycles of societies where radical breakthroughs or destruction are likely to occur," Michael Fullan writes in *Change Forces*. "Teachers' capacities to deal with change, learn from it, and help students learn from it will be critical for the future development of societies. They are not now in a position to play this vital role. We need a new mindset to go deeper."[1]

To Martin Diego, the Gladston education partnership's executive director who was observing the training session that day, the issue comes down to dollars and sense. "We could spend ten million dollars of the Davidsons' money and come up with nothing," he told the teachers. "It's possible to do that. Is ten million dollars enough to transform what you're planning at this time and in this way? That's the big question."

These discussions were part of an intensive three-day workshop scheduled for the first full week of July 1999, which represented the first time the newly hired faculty members of the Gladston Regional Campus project's freshman academy and business academy were able to meet and begin shaping their experimental programs. For these educators, the task was both exhilarating and overwhelming. They had to find ways to keep disengaged students from dropping out of school, construct assignments and tests that would enable all students to reach higher standards of learning, and build a school culture that would encourage both adolescents and adults to focus on continuous improvement — objectives that most urban schools in America have failed to meet.

While they were dreaming of these bold achievements, the teachers and administrator also had to work around some obstacles to enlightenment. They had less than two months — from the time they were hired to the time the doors of the new school buildings opened — to learn how to work with each other and with the 423 students who had signed up for the two academies. The Davidson grant paid for eleven days of specialized training that summer, but each participant received a stipend of only $60 a day, the school district's approved daily compensation rate for professional development. And because the district requires teachers to spend only two days a year in continuing education, none of the academy faculty members could be compelled to attend the summer sessions. Although most did show up, some teachers could not participate in every session because of conflicts with child-care arrangements, college courses they needed for certification, and summer jobs they had committed to work.

Despite these limitations, the faculties were expected to quickly move from introductions to interdependence. That was the lofty goal of the summer training program, whose daily themes ranged from "Vision and Beliefs" and "Norms, Roles, and Relationships" to "Focus on Results — Standards" and "Inventing Quality Work." The new staff members, who started with trust-building exercises and evolved to designing actual lesson plans together, had to critique their products according to well-defined criteria, then revise them again and again until they got them right. The process showed them just how hard it is to put grand ideas into action.

Take collaboration and trust, for example. After spending a hot day participating in an outdoor obstacle climbing exercise set up to help organizations develop greater teamwork and camaraderie, the teachers discussed their reactions. Veteran high school English teacher Ellen Jackson complimented a younger colleague for her willingness to show her partners that she needed to be sure of their support before she was willing to climb to the top of a precipice.

"I thought, 'You go, girl,'" Jackson said. "You knew your limits and you weren't afraid to set them."

English teacher Sidney Mound said he thought the activities would have been more effective if the participants had gotten to know each other better before they were required to join forces. The quick, forced intimacy did not make people immediately comfortable or confident in each other, he said.

"I know what you mean," said Doris Eickmeyer, who had tried to implement team teaching and interdisciplinary studies when she taught social studies at Lincoln High School. She said the outdoor team activities reminded her of the first time she saw her husband undressed except for his boxer shorts and she thought, "Okay, I guess this is for good."

The group erupted in laughter. Married or not, they could relate to her vivid description. Collaborative teaching does strip away some of the protections that educators typically use to keep themselves from feeling exposed — and, therefore, vulnerable — outside the closed classroom. The new freshman academy faculty believed that they might gain support, new ideas, and richer instruction by working together, but many feared moving into the educational equivalent of a fishbowl, where every action could be scrutinized and, potentially, criticized.

"We not only have to create the environment of trust between us, we have to teach the kids how to be that way for each other," said Gary Rosenberger, a soft-spoken, earnest math teacher.

Janey Lewis, program leader of the freshman academy, expanded on Rosenberger's thoughtful reflection by urging the faculty to remember the anxiety of their team-building exercises when they began trying to develop relationships with their students.

"How do we create an atmosphere in a classroom — a safe environment — so that kids know, 'Everyone here wants me to grow'?" she asked them.

Hummel reminded the group that in any organization — including schools — there are five different types of people, all of whom contribute to the change process in both positive and negative ways. The first type, the "trailblazers," loves to explore, to chart new paths, and to experience change. In education, these people are the first to sign up for professional development courses or to try new instructional techniques with little direction. However, they also can become extremely impatient with people who don't adapt as quickly as they do, and before everyone has perfected the process, they itch to try the next new thing.

The second group, the "pioneers," includes individuals who are adventuresome and capable of taking risks but who need to clearly understand the purpose of a new agenda before they agree to pursue it.

The third group, the largest, is called the "settlers." People in this category need detailed explanations of the reasons for change, specific examples of how to change, and constant reinforcement while they're trying to change. In education, settlers want to see samples of successful lessons, not just broad curriculum goals. "They want to be sure they know how to do what will be required of them. Indeed, many potential settlers will not move until they have assurances that the requisite knowledge and support are available to them," Phillip Schlechty, president of the Center for Leadership in School Reform, writes. "Perhaps the most critical thing to remember about settlers is that they need strong, constant, and reassuring leadership that inspires them to keep going when they are tempted to turn back."[2]

The fourth type is called the "stay-at-homes." This group usually doesn't actively defy the proposed restructuring plan, but members won't easily accept it either. They are passive resisters of change. If the pressure to conform becomes too great, many stay-at-homes will choose to leave the school or the profession rather than adapt.

The final group is called the "saboteurs," individuals who fight the reforms and wait for them to fail so they can say, 'I told you so.' "Saboteurs' favorite strategy is to sow distrust through rumors and disinformation, and they will destroy even the best organized wagon train if they can gain enough followers," Schlechty writes. "Certainly, saboteurs can be disruptive, and some will not cooperate even enough to communicate their concerns. If, however, change leaders continue to reach out to saboteurs and critics and try hard to hear what they are saying, sometimes there is much to be learned. It might be learned that some saboteurs were once trailblazers and pioneers who at some time in the past had the misfortune to follow leaders who did not give them the support they needed and abandoned them at the first sign of trouble."[3]

As a practical matter, Hummel told the staffs of the freshman and business academies, they had to be careful not to alienate educators at the two existing high schools lest they "get their backs up and become saboteurs" who keep the recommended reforms from spreading throughout the district. "You've got to break down the barriers between 'we' and 'they.'"

Hummel suggested that one of the best ways to win converts was to improve the content and style of instruction so reluctant teachers couldn't help but notice and appreciate the difference. To start with, she encouraged them to focus on the big ideas — such as "What should students know at the end of ninth grade?" — and work backward to the actual lessons that would help students understand them.

"People tend to talk about kids as products — things we mold and shape," Hummel said, adding that the Center for Leadership in School Reform tries to reframe the conversation to talk about students "as customers who bring their own needs and interests to the process. The work we give them becomes the way we satisfy the needs of our primary customers." States can compel students to attend school until they are sixteen, Hummel said, but teenagers "will not commit to the work" unless they enjoy learning or see some payoff from what teachers ask them to do. "Their attendance can be commanded, but their attention must be earned."

For those who would scoff at the notion of schools changing to fit the students instead of the other way around, Hummel would remind them that back in the so-called "good old days" of the 1950s and 1960s, half the teenagers in the United States did not graduate from high school. Therefore, it wasn't too difficult for teachers to "turn on" those who stayed. Three or four decades ago, students also had fewer distractions. Today, students have video games, computers, twenty-four-hour-a-day television, and after-school jobs, among other things that compete for their attention.

To hold students' interest, Hummel said, modern-day teachers have to connect what they are doing *inside* the classroom to what teenagers see *outside* it. In other words, they need to design work that students consider relevant and challenging, assignments in which they can actively participate, not just passively observe. "Kids will persist with work if they can create a product they value," Hummel said.

One teacher said the shift in emphasis reminded him of his experience working at a discount store during the Christmas holidays. He learned about the retail strategy of putting items at the end of store aisles to grab the attention of impulse buyers, people who would see the products and say, 'Gee, I didn't know I needed this.' In the same way, he said, teachers can get students to "buy" key concepts and skills by making the lesson so appealing that they are drawn to them.

"The only thing over which teachers have control is the work they design," Hummel said in agreement. "They can't control the kids or their families or their incomes."

Although teachers can't control students' personal issues, they have to deal with the repercussions just the same. Creating interesting and challenging assignments is not as easy as it might sound, particularly when one's prior experience as a teacher — before that, as a student — has focused on taking an activity that someone else created and passing it on. During one of the summer training sessions, the business academy staff members worked together to conceive a project in which students would be asked to create a viable product and plan an advertising campaign to market it, using actual rates for media buys. Staff members decided that the students also would have to present their proposals to a local advertising firm whose representatives would help evaluate the quality of their work. After about fifteen minutes, however, the staff's enthusiasm for the proposed project waned. One young teacher got angry when she realized that the group expected *her* to make a presentation about the project to the others later that day. Her reaction suggested that she would have a difficult time modeling the public speaking skills she expected her students to develop. Another teacher said he didn't understand how the marketing project met the academic standards they were supposed to address.

"We just went through and designed this," acknowledged Al Gazortz, instructional leader of the business academy. "Probably what we should have done is find the standard and work backward to the project.... We should be asking, 'Why are we creating this?' Because if you can't design a project to meet a standard, you might as well not do it."

In another section of the room, a group of English teachers discussed how to encourage students to write stronger paragraphs by integrating the lessons with literature studies. For example, students would learn about the concept of love in literary works such as *Romeo and Juliet* and *Great Expectations*, then write short essays examining certain themes that emerged from the literature, such as "love is painful." A teacher suggested letting students work in pairs to come up with five examples of each theme from the literary works they had studied. Later, with the whole class reassembled, the students could debate whether the examples were specific or general.

A group of math teachers designed a project to reinforce the geometry concepts of length and width. By asking students to create a floor plan for an apartment they'd like to rent, the teachers said they hoped to demonstrate the importance of understanding basic computations, graphing, ratios, and proportions. One teacher suggested bringing in building contractors to talk to the students about practical applications of math, such as how much area a gallon of paint would cover and how they could determine equivalent quantities when moving between yards and gallons.

After each group had finished describing its project, the teachers discussed how the proposed lessons did or did not meet the Center for Leadership in School Reform's ten definitions of "quality work." Among the definitions they considered:

Content and substance — Are the ideas, propositions, facts, and insights that are presented consistent with those generally agreed upon by scholars in those disciplines?

Product focus — Do students understand the connection between what they are doing and what they are expected to produce?

Clear and compelling product standards — Are the standards by which the products or the performances are to be assessed clearly articulated?

Protection from initial failures — Are students provided feedback throughout the project other than at grade time?[4]

This critiquing process, which the academy faculties began in the summer of 1999, continued throughout the next school year. From lesson plans to student discipline to team relationships, the teachers' efforts to raise the bar for themselves and their students was examined from multiple angles. They might have received more financial and interpersonal supports than educators typically do, but no one was going to cut them any slack just because they were new to the school reform process. The pressure to produce would come from all quarters: the school system that was timidly following their direction, the foundations that had paid them to improve, the parents who had entrusted their children to the new school designs, and the colleagues who wondered whether they also would have to change their expectations and practices to keep pace.

As summer faded, the staffs of the freshman academy and business academy publicly acted prepared and ready to start their new roles. Privately, they worried about many issues. Had they received enough training, and was it the right combination of theory and practice? Could they trust the recommendations to dramatically alter their instruction, knowing they wouldn't have clear evidence that the innovations were working until much later in the school year? Would the school district and the larger community give them adequate support and time to demonstrate the potential of their new model? Could they depend on their leaders — Lewis and Gazortz — to provide sufficient guidance as they attempted to change gears?

Some of their concerns were technical in nature, but all depended on the human side of school change. Take the issue of working within teams. During the last week of the summer training, Lewis and Dean of Students Scott Peterson assigned the freshman academy teachers to various groups. Four teams consisted of core subject teachers — social studies, English, math, and science — whereas the teachers of technology, family and consumer sciences, special education, math intervention, and career exploration would be assigned to work either with two of the four teams or rotate among all of them throughout the school year. A guidance counselor also was available to assist any student who needed help and to coordinate course scheduling with Jefferson and Lincoln high schools.

When the core teachers heard the names of their partners, some were not pleased. Although most of the staff dutifully accepted the assignments, one teacher exploded. She said she could not work with one of her team members, a teacher with whom she had previously taught and whom she considered condescending. Lewis became equally adamant and refused to reconfigure the teams to accommodate personal differences. It was the first test of her resolve, and she stood her ground, taking the affected team members away from the training room to resolve the complaint. The disgruntled teacher reluctantly capitulated, but she and others remained wary.

To Lewis, the choice was clear: the needs of students must come before the demands of teachers. "The whole thing was based on helping kids to succeed in high school, in life, in career choice," she said later. "If you expect teachers to team teach, there will be dysfunctional teams. I mean, even in the best-functioning teams that we have, I know that I have personality clashes.... Sometimes I think human nature tends to want to have somebody that you can dislike or be irritated with. Because it's easier to have somebody to blame than to have to deal" with your own problems.

Lewis said she wasn't trying to minimize the difficulty of working with other people, particularly with the community's spotlight bringing every interaction into closer view. But she believed the planned collaborations were possible, and she was-n't about to concede defeat before the staff of the freshman academy had started working together.

"I try to be really understanding and try to put myself in their position because the layers of change and reform that we're asking of these people are so overwhelming," Lewis said. "I'm sure there are probably going to be those who don't feel that this is a good fit for them. I think that's where the greatest conster-nation has come with some of the staff and me, because my vision...from the beginning has been that we wanted this to be a place for success for kids.

"We are the creators of the work, and it's incumbent on us, if we're not getting to them one way, we've got to change the way we're approaching it."

IO

TEACHING ON DISPLAY

Wearing a white lab coat, squinting through a pair of safety goggles, and standing behind a table filled with glass cylinders, chemicals, and measuring tools, Leticia Herron looked every bit the part of a scientist carefully preparing an experiment. But to the sixteen ninth-graders seated before her at the freshman academy, she was just a science teacher in a costume, and they were in no mood to pretend.

Four times in the first five minutes of class, she tried to explain how to determine the effectiveness of various antacids in neutralizing stomach acids. And each time, she was interrupted by questions from students, some of whom were genuinely confused by the procedure Herron was demonstrating and others who were purposely trying to disrupt the lesson.

"If you spill this stuff on your clothes, you'll be sorry," Herron warned as she showed them how to weigh and measure the solutions. "You need to listen to the directions."

She pointed to a flip chart where she had written out the procedure for testing three different antacids in different amounts. Students also could read the same information from a worksheet she had distributed two days before.

"If you're going to be smart aleck today and insist on asking questions, I am going to have to ask you to leave because I can't have that and acids," she told one student.

A small, instense, bespectacled woman, Herron is as precise as some of her students are lackadaisical. Passionate about her subject, she had spent hours preparing a lesson that she assumed her students would love as much as she did. But there were some problems. The freshmen didn't know *why* they were conducting the experiment. They didn't understand *how*. And some of them assumed from past failures in school that they were incapable of doing it well.

About ten minutes after the start of the class, when she thought the students were ready, Herron divided them into small groups. Students donned vinyl aprons and goggles, collected their equipment, and began the experiment.

"I like when you measure correctly. It shows you're paying attention," she encouraged one student as she circulated among the tables.

"Josh and Jeremy, are you working?" she asked a fidgety duo.

"Here's the deal. Keep looking. Keep listening," she called out to the whole class. "If you have acid on the table, you must have goggles on. We only have thirty minutes today. You guys have to stay on task."

Clumsy in his preparations, Josh spilled some of the Congo red indicator on his hand and rushed to the sink to rinse it.

"It's not coming off," he shouted.

"Josh, I told you it will come off in a few minutes," Herron said calmly. "I washed my hands twice this morning and it came off."

"I want it off now!" he yelled.

"Maybe you need to go sit in the hall because I need to teach this class," Herron shot back, her voice edgy.

Josh continued washing his hands but said no more. A few minutes later, he returned to the table and resumed the experiment with his partner. Suddenly, the two students jumped back from the table, trying to avoid being stained by the Congo red indicator that was flooding the table. "Oh, man, what a retard," Jeremy yelled at him, trying to wipe up the blood-red stain with a wad of paper towels.

"Ms. Herron, Ms. Herron," irrepressible students vied for her attention from all around the room.

Josh walked over to the sink, looking for more Congo red indicator to replace what he had spilled. Herron told him there was no more solution. Jeremy removed his safety goggles and wandered around the room, checking out the action at other tables.

"Jeremy, if you can't keep your goggles on, you'll need to leave the room," Herron said, turning away from the student she was helping so she could bring Jeremy back into focus.

Jeremy said nothing and walked into the hall.

"So you've made a decision to get a zero on this assignment," Herron said, her comment making a statement more than asking a question.

Without speaking, Jeremy walked back into the classroom, sat on his stool, and strapped the goggles back on.

Another minute or two passed without incident.

"Ooh, it smells minty," a girl observed as she sniffed a beaker and stirred. "It should," Herron told her pleasantly, excited by the student's interest in the details of the experiment. "That's what antacids smell like."

Just then her gaze reverted to Josh and Jeremy's table. Seeing another disaster in the making, Macala exploded like the chemical reactions she was trying to contain. She marched over to their table and told Josh to go call his mother from a telephone in the office. He refused. "I was following directions," he said, pouting.

Her face flushed with frustration, Herron walked out of the classroom, calling over her shoulder: "People, Mr. Mound is going to be your supervisor for about two minutes."

Sidney Mound, an English teacher and one of four teachers on Herron's team, had been helping a student at a computer in the back of the double-sized classroom. As he walked forward to take charge of the class, he paused to correct a student who was making a disturbance. "You are a very bright person," he said. "You're just a hemorrhoid."

"Hey, Mr. Dude," another student called out jovially as Mound passed by on his way to the front of the classroom.

"Mr. Dude?" Mound barked back. "I am a teacher. Respect me at all times."

A few minutes later, Herron returned to the classroom, followed by Scott Peterson, the dean of students at the freshman academy. Peterson conferred with Josh, then Jeremy, then Herron. When Josh left the classroom again to go to the office, Jeremy joined another group of students to finish the experiment.

At the conclusion of the class, Herron asked the students to clean up their tables and keep their worksheets until the following day.

"That was a groovy experiment," a student called out casually as she sashayed out of the room.

When the room was empty, Herron stayed behind to finish cleaning up the lab. Her jaw tight and her brow furrowed, she quietly wiped a table, looking frustrated and angry. Peterson walked back into the room, and Herron turned to him with obvious anger, demanding that he suspend Josh from school.

"That's not going to happen, Leticia," Peterson said neutrally, explaining that he had directed Josh to write a reflection about the class and meet with him and Herron the following day.

Afterward, in private, Peterson said he believed that Herron had overreacted to the situation. His take was that the students' behavior had been disrespectful, which had hurt Herron's feelings, so she initially responded from the point of pain before carefully diagnosing the reason for the ensuing chaos. The students had been confused, Peterson said, and he was concerned that Herron seemed more intent on getting to the end of the experiment than in answering their questions fully and directly.

"The good news is that Leticia, after she cools down, is really able to see these things," Peterson said. "She's a hard worker, and that kid *is* a clown. He can get under your skin. And partly, the science curriculum is very challenging. The kids really have a hard time with labs."

Later that day, when Herron ran through the same experiment on acids and bases with a different class of freshmen, the results were about the same. The second time, she demonstrated the procedure by directing a student assistant at her side, but his classmates paid no more attention than the first group.

"Jessica, if you can't be polite, you need to leave the room," Herron admonished a student whose outbursts had become obnoxious. "There's no need to be rude."

When a boy began singing out loud, Herron walked over to his table and quietly asked him to stop.

"We need to be doing this instead of having only one person do it," the boy said, sulking.

Herron explained that the first class had been careless with the dangerous acids and that she wanted to take more precautions this time. She repeated the steps of the procedure, but the students were still confused, so she created a chart on the dry erase board in the front of the room.

Later, when most of the students were quietly conducting the experiment, a handful of them continued disrupting the class, shrieking, shouting, and keeping everyone from concentrating. Peterson stood in the doorway for a few minutes, and the chatter quickly stilled.

With Herron's permission, math teacher Kyran Larkin had set up a video recorder in the back of the classroom so she could tape the lesson. The two colleagues, who work together on the same teaching team, often record their lessons so they can review them later and find ways to improve their instruction.

"Why are you taping us?" a student asked as she peered into the camera lens.

"So I can show it to your parents to talk to them about your behavior," Larkin said with obvious irritation.

As the class time ticked away, Herron asked some probing questions, hoping to get the students to think analytically about the scientific data they had collected, but few of them were engaged in the activity. Peterson continued walking in and out of the classroom, trying to use his presence to keep the students on track. At one point, he removed a boy who had gotten out his new yearbook and was passing it around for signatures.

The class and the school day ended a short time later, but not before Herron wondered what she had done wrong. She had started the year full of optimism, promising the students on the first day of school that none of them would fail. "All of you are going to the tenth grade," she had told them with obvious sincerity. "You *will* be successful here."

As it turned out, seven students on her team failed for the year. Although not the highest number among the freshman academy's four teams, the total was more than Herron or anyone else wanted or anticipated.

The reasons for the disappointing results were rooted in both personal and pedagogical issues. Herron had not counted on having one teammate whose emotional problems frequently spilled over into the classroom and another who refused to collaborate on lessons or stay a minute past the dismissal bell. She had not counted on having students whose academic preparation for serious scientific inquiry was so weak that they had no concept of proper laboratory procedures, much less the scientific process of making inferences, controlling for variables, and testing hypotheses. She had not counted on having her methods of instilling structure and discipline in the classroom so often challenged by students and other teachers at the freshman academy. And she had not counted on having to constantly analyze her instructional strategies, searching for clues to why they missed the mark with many students.

Her experiences — sometimes more humbling than triumphant — show just how hard it is to improve teaching and learning in urban high schools. Herron is typical of teachers who were trained to use one dominant mode of instruction —

and did so with success — but now must learn a variety of new methods while simultaneously keeping up with the traditional job responsibilities, from grading homework to designing tests. Though she often struggled to meet the diverse needs of her students, Herron's supervisors said she worked harder at refining her practices and was more open to change than many of her colleagues. She routinely submitted outlines of her lessons to Judy Hummel, the coach from the Center for Leadership in School Reform, and sought advice from Peterson and freshman academy Program Leader Janey Lewis. She made sure her fellow science teachers met on a regular basis to share ideas and coordinate their lessons, personally putting in long hours after school and on weekends trying to keep all of them on track. She attended professional conferences and classes and read everything she could get her hands on about developing more effective instructional techniques.

Yet, while some teachers seem to instinctively possess interpersonal and instructional skills that enable them to relate easily to teenagers and persuade them to learn difficult subject matter, Herron had a tough time connecting her obvious intellectual gifts to the varied preparation and interest of her students. Like Patrick Alton at Jefferson High School, she falls into that class of teachers whom education reformers must find a way to reach — those who are very willing to improve but haven't had enough opportunity to figure out how.

"Most teachers do not demonstrate" an instructional repertoire that is consistently engaging for students, Patricia

Wasley and her colleagues at Bank Street College of Education discovered in a three-year study of high school students. "When we asked teachers whether they had a repertoire of *approaches* [emphasis added] for working with kids, most said yes — and then described *curriculum* [emphasis added] as the source of their repertoire: 'First I teach different organisms, then body parts, then the different systems within the body.... It's tough to fit it all in.' What they lacked was the corresponding variation in pedagogical and assessment strategies. Curriculum — whatever the subject — was the renewable resource providing teachers with new and fresh stimulation. They assumed that variation within the curriculum would sustain their students. Unfortunately, the sameness of the days weighed heavily on the kids."[1]

Herron provides a case in point. Trained to follow more traditional lecture-intensive teaching techniques, she said the additional training she had received as a faculty member of the freshman academy had persuaded her to change her habits.

"I always knew there was a better way, but I didn't know what it was," she said. "I used to be a 'talking head.' I'm aware of that now. I'm sort of embarrassed that I used to teach that way. I mean, I used to do labs, but when I wasn't doing that I was talking *at* them. It was boring for my kids and I knew it, but I didn't know what to do about it. Now I know that there's a lot I have to do to make learning happen for my students."

During the first year of a difficult transition in a new school building with new team members and new students, she wasn't able to consistently connect the innovative theories she had discovered with the daily practices in her classroom. The chaotic experiment with acids and bases, for example, occurred during the last month of the school year.

Other experiments turned out well, however. For example, earlier in the school year she had enthralled the same group of students with an investigation of energy and motion. The discussion ranged from oceans and wave patterns to the effect of wind on land and water. As Herron demonstrated the properties of shock waves using a giant Slinky and a metal coil, the students watched intently. The lesson was fun. The toy she used was one most of the students had played with as young children, and Herron made sure it was large enough so that all of them could see the experiment from anywhere in the room. As a result, the freshmen stayed focused during the entire class period, frequently shouting out intelligent observations and answers to Herron's questions.

At other times, when Herron was able to work one-on-one with students or in small groups, she was able to reach them and her intensity seemed to be an asset. But many days, she came to class almost overly prepared, intent on completing her planned lessons. Her drive was admirable, but it sometimes caused her to miss the step of finding out what her students knew and needed to know to gain mastery of a topic. As a result, she sometimes failed to adjust the activities to help her students comprehend difficult material. In turn, many of them misbehaved rather than acknowledge their ignorance.

Take the antacid experiment. Instead of trying to complete

a complicated investigation with multiple steps and variable equations, she might have tried breaking down the objectives into smaller segments so students could follow the steps more easily. She might have found ways to connect the topic to the students' experiences by replaying a taped television commercial for a popular stomach antacid, showing them how the digestive process works with a see-through dummy, or letting students evaluate the effectiveness of antacids on their own bodies after eating spicy foods.

"You live and learn in a program like this," Herron acknowledged.

Hummel said designing challenging and engaging lessons is not only the best way to help students learn but is also the best way to improve discipline in a school. But many teachers can't make the connection, she said. They blame the students for being unruly, call them unfocused and lazy, yet don't see how other instructors can work with the same teenagers and achieve far different results. She recalled visiting the classroom of one freshman academy teacher and asking him about that day's lesson. When he said he was teaching about an old and obscure drama, Hummel asked him whether the students had expressed interest in knowing more about the play. "He said, 'No, not at all.' I said, 'Why are you doing it then?' He said, 'Because I acted in the play in college.' That says so much. He thinks he's designing work that's interesting to kids. He's not."

Showing teachers *how* — not just *why* — they should design lessons that include meaningful topics and choices for students would be the focus of the staff development during the summer of 2000 and beyond, Hummel promised as she reviewed the experiences of the freshman academy's first year with teachers, administrators, and students. In a letter that she sent to the staff on May 12, 2000, she outlined some of the essential features of good assignments:

- Generally, a unit of work should not exceed three weeks.
- Generally, one needs to build in class time for project work that involves teams of students.
- Generally, there is the need to develop a written outline of the work that will be assigned to students that includes, but is not limited to, the following elements — results to be achieved; the products that need to be developed; [and] a time line when different aspects of the work need to be completed.
- Generally, students should not be assigned more than three or four in-depth projects in a grading period, and they need to be spaced so that projects are not due at the same time and do not require the use of the same technologies.
- Generally, one needs to build in time for students to have work reviewed and/or practice time before a performance or final product is due.[2]

It wasn't clear whether Herron could adapt her instruction accordingly. But far from being disillusioned by her inconsistent success connecting with students during the first year of the freshman academy, she believed that with continued coaching and support she would be much more effective during the second year. She talked excitedly about the strong professional relationship she had forged with Kyran Larkin. The two had spent a lot of time taking advanced education courses, sharing ideas, and working together to make various instructional and scheduling improvements. Herron also credited Lewis for using her leadership skills to help the staff grow on the job.

"Janey's wonderful," Herron said. "She has taught me more than I've learned in my teaching career…partly because I was willing to listen."

Scott Peterson, who said Herron's eagerness to improve set her apart from many of her colleagues, was another supervisor whom she was counting on to help. On the day of the failed experiment on acids and bases, he took time to meet after school with Herron and Larkin, extending emotional support to the two women while subtly coaching them in the art of effective instruction and classroom management.

"This is one of my best labs," Herron said to Peterson. "I knew I didn't have much time to fit it in. I guess I came in a little nervous today."

Peterson reassured her. "This isn't about your lesson," he said. "This is a team issue."

The four members of Herron's team had not established good rapport and consistent discipline policies early in the school year, he said, and disruptive students took advantage of the loose boundaries. To illustrate his point, he said he had removed the most rebellious and outspoken student on the team after the first grading period, placed her with another group of teachers, "and she hasn't been to the office since."

Having said that, Peterson recognized that it was still possible for Herron to refine her techniques and achieve good results. He encouraged her to redo the lab experiment on acids and bases the following day, but this time clearly breaking down the steps of the investigation and showing students how to succeed with the lesson.

"Tell the kids, 'We're going to do this until you get it right,'" he said to Herron. "That's what standards are all about."

"I think that's a great idea," Herron said, laughing with relief. "I never would have come to that place myself. I was ready to put the whole thing away."

"When you redo the lab, I'll come in and sit with the kids. You do the lab and I'll do the bull session," Peterson offered, adding that he thought all four of the science teachers in the freshman academy needed such assistance. "Our curriculum person designed this [laboratory] sequence for upper-end kids, and you're teaching lower-end kids who have no experience with this."

Herron hugged him when he reminded her that "it's going to be so much better next year." The tension seemed to drain from her face for the first time that day.

"I can't tell you how much I appreciate your coming in here to go over this," Herron said, beaming.

She released Peterson and, after he and Larkin left, resumed straightening the room, planning tomorrow's activities in her mind. It would be a new day, and Leticia Herron would have another chance to get it right.

II

WHERE EVERYBODY
KNOWS YOUR NAME

Teaching urban high school students is
not for those who quickly back down
from challenges, as Leticia Herron's
experience shows. Americans still like to think
of a high school classroom as a Norman
Rockwell painting come alive. A stern but
benevolent teacher stands in front of the classroom, the flag unfurls above a chalkboard filled
with perfect penmanship, and the students sit in
their neat rows of desks and listen attentively as
she speaks. The view is pure nostalgia, not a
reality in Gladston, or most other communities
across the nation.

What today's high school teachers see
when they look out at the sea of students is a
hodgepodge of hormones, hairstyles, and
heredity. They also see reflections of what lies
beneath: abuse, fear, optimism, pain, alienation,

distrust, confidence, failure, and a wide range of characteristics and attitudes born of the experiences that each person has been fortunate to experience or forced to endure.

It isn't fair to pigeonhole urban high school students. Many come from good homes, try hard in school, and move through life without generating controversy. But their opposites are well represented, too. Such students test authority, sabotage the progress of their peers, confound their advocates, and engage in as many risky behaviors as necessary to blot out the hurt and disappointment in their lives. They don't know how to relate to other people, how to dress for public functions, how to stick with something past the point of frustration, or how to apply for a job. One freshman academy teacher refers to the worst of them as "haters," students who walk in the classroom so full of misery and rage that they attack first and count their victims later.

The freshman academy faculty not only accepted the challenge of teaching 330 members of this widely divergent group, but also promised to become so involved in their lives that no one would be left behind. The emphasis on relationships was supposed to be one of the distinguishing features of the academy, in the words of Program Leader Janey Lewis, "a place where everybody knows your name." More precisely, it was supposed to be a place where everybody knows your business — who your friends are, how well you are performing in English class, and whether you ate supper the night before.

To outsiders who hear her promoting the academy's ideals,

Lewis's mantra can sound as trite as an inspirational slogan painted on posters and coffee mugs. She tries to ignore those skeptics. Lewis knows that although students have a legal obligation to attend school until age sixteen, they will not listen or learn unless they connect to the heart of a high school.

"Some people think this is just about academic results, but it's not," Lewis said halfway through the first semester. "We've fed kids who've come to school hungry. We're dealing with the whole person. There are human issues — emotional, mental, physical. We have to deal with those first and convince them [the students] that we care."

Research backs up her views. The Search Institute, a national nonprofit organization that works to promote healthy adolescent development, reviewed data from thousands of student surveys throughout the country and concluded that "schools that nurture positive relationships among students and among students and teachers are more likely to realize the payoff of more engaged students achieving at higher levels."[1]

Expanding on this research in the book *Great Places to Learn: How Asset-Building Schools Help Students Succeed*, adolescent development specialists Neal Starkman, Peter Scales, and Clay Roberts said they found consistent data that academic success is strongly related to a student's social competence and adaptability to various environments. The critical response from schools is a combination of emotional caring and intellectual challenge.[2]

"Students with such skills and attitudes as stress management, self-control, self-direction, and personal responsibility have high academic achievement levels," the three wrote. "This leads some researchers to say that student progress on social competence, even more than intellectual measures, 'might be the best primary measure' of academic success."[3]

Many freshman academy students don't have the attributes that Starkman and his colleagues talk about in *Great Places to Learn* because they have had such unpredictable parenting and uneven educational experiences.

"These kids are so shortsighted," science teacher Adam Hynes explained one day. "Their horizon is so limited because of their urban environment or their home. It's like being in a whiteout. They're so used to looking at their toes, they can't see there's more out there. They have very little outside perspective."

To fully understand their students, the freshman academy educators looked to the Search Institute for guidance. The organization has developed a prescription of forty essential building blocks that adolescents need to successfully navigate the course from dependent teenagers to self-sufficient, socially responsible adults. These "developmental assets" include basic foundations that begin at home, such as a personal commitment to learning, attention to positive values, socialization skills, and a positive identity. "Internal assets" need to be bolstered by an outside infrastructure called "external assets," including parental involvement in children's personal and academic lives, a strong neighborhood environment, and a community that endorses and provides its youth with consistent boundaries and expectations.

Scott Peterson, dean of students at the freshman academy,

had hoped that all of the ninth-graders would be able to complete a survey, "Search Institute Profiles of Student Life: Attitudes and Behaviors," at the beginning and end of the 1999–2000 school year so the staff could compare the results. He also had counted on comparing the freshman academy students with a "control" group of nonacademy ninth-graders, following both groups over four years to see if the freshman academy practices had expanded the students' developmental assets. However, with so many competing demands to get the faculty trained and the new building opened on schedule, there wasn't time to identify the two groups. Freshman academy students did not complete the Search Institute survey until the end of the 1999–2000 school year, which made Peterson's desired comparisons impossible.

The survey results — which the school received in September 2000 — confirmed what Peterson, Hynes, and many others had surmised: Most freshman academy students don't have adequate assets, either internal or external. On average, the freshman class of 1999–2000 had only eighteen of the forty assets in their lives. Fewer than twenty students reported having more than thirty assets, which is the ideal *minimum* according to researchers.

"We were particularly deficient in the area of community support that exists in our town *for kids*," Peterson said of the survey results. "We have this great community turnout when you have sporting events...but when you talk about members of the community mentoring kids and having an adult besides your parent that you really connect with, we were particularly deficient."

The results also showed *how* assets matter. Students who reported having ten or fewer assets experienced triple the average number of high-risk behaviors — such as drug and alcohol use, cigarette smoking, sexual relationships, violence, and truancy — as did students with twenty-one to thirty assets. The survey also showed that the students who have the fewest assets engage in only half the number of positive behaviors as their asset-rich peers. Positive behaviors include maintaining good health habits, avoiding dangerous activities, engaging in leadership roles, and succeeding academically, among others.

Although they didn't receive this detailed information until the start of the second school year, the freshman academy faculty members followed their earlier hunches and began providing extra support services to students at the beginning of the pilot year. Some of those services came in the form of cultural field trips to theatrical productions where students had to dress appropriately and learn proper etiquette. They also visited work sites and local college campuses to understand what the world beyond high school looks like. And teachers helped organize formal meals, including a Thanksgiving dinner at the academy, so these teenagers — many had never eaten anywhere better than a fast-food joint — could learn various social graces, such as how to set a table and seat guests.

Lewis said teachers intentionally set up the meals inside the academy because "the schoolhouse is supposed to be a safe place…for those kids who didn't know [appropriate social behaviors] it was a place to save face."

Students seemed to appreciate the sum of their combined academic and social experiences. "I learned to be respectful of my elders," one student said of his year at the freshman academy. "And how to be responsible and how to be with people other than my friends."

"I learned that everything doesn't go your way, and you can't just quit," another student said upon reflection.

The freshman academy "is harder than Jefferson," said Jeremy, a sixteen-year-old freshman, without any hint of complaint. Freshman academy teachers "expect more of you. You have more responsibility here."

The freshman academy staff members believe these comments showed that students were learning good "people skills" through strong relationships with adults they trusted. Although the educators did not succeed in reaching every student during the pilot year, the end-of-the-year results would show that they made extraordinary progress with many kids.

"It's a different kind of school here," acknowledged Zack, a freshman who frequently tested the limits of the faculty's pledge to help every student succeed. "They care about kids. I like it."

That endorsement didn't come from a teenager whom anybody would be glad to teach. Zack was one of the toughest turnarounds the staff attempted. By the end of the first semester, he was failing many of his classes, moving to a new teaching team because of so many discipline infractions on the first one, and threatening to give up or blow up nearly every day. But no matter how hard he struggled or spun out of control, he never felt ignored. Unlike the class at his home high school that he admittedly slept through without interference from the teacher, Zack knew that the adults at the freshman academy would not let him slip by.

"That wouldn't happen here," he said with a knowing grin.

Many of Zack's classmates admitted sleeping through or skipping classes at their home high schools but said they didn't try the same stunts at the freshman academy. Part of the reason is that with no more than 175 students in attendance in the morning or afternoon sessions, the freshman academy was small enough to feel close-knit. Absent students were noticed and missed. Teachers also moved beyond traditional classroom duties by calling students' parents, visiting students at home, working with them after school, and counseling them throughout the day, trying any strategy they could think of to overcome the indifference that drives students to drop out, or figuratively check out, of school.

"I like the support the teachers give you," said fifteen-year-old Tameka. "If you need something, they don't brush you off...they help you; they don't put you down. It's so many people there [at her home high school] that they don't notice you. You have to do something for the whole school before they notice you. Like here, at the freshman academy, some girl, her mother died, and they gave her condolences, and they told us when the funeral would be. That was nice."

The freshman academy leaders believe, and research confirms, that when students such as Tameka feel demeaned, dismissed, or denied a voice in their educational experiences, they often detach themselves from the process entirely. And although many teenagers are loath to admit it, they prefer a school in which the adults monitor their whereabouts.

"Many of the students I know…do not have this sense of a school community backing them up. Too many of my peers don't think that they matter.…. This is what they need most, just to be bombarded with the idea that people do care," Colorado high school senior Sara Pierce wrote in the foreword to *Great Places to Learn*. "Very rarely will students turn away from the opportunity to form connections or become involved, if they are invited and made to feel welcome.…. School must be more than just a place to learn…it should be a place to belong."[4]

That's a commonsense message, but putting it into practice is hard work. Many high school students are so far behind in what educated people consider appropriate emotional and intellectual development that it's almost impossible to reach them without assigning (and paying) more adults to work in schools. These students need people who can provide a range of related services, from mentoring to modeling manners. Like it or not, many teenagers today never learned why school is important. In a me-first society that so often puts immediate gratification ahead of long-term goals, many young people don't know why they should bother to build a record of academic achievement. They hear of college dropouts who became Internet millionaires or sports superstars who bypassed college for the pros, yet they don't stop to consider the odds against the same things happening to them. Or they see drug dealers drive by the neighborhood in expensive cars, but don't think about the prison terms or violence that also come with the job.

These attitudes can be particularly maddening to teachers who not only learned to honor educational distinction, they joined a profession that would enable them to pass those same values on to others. It frustrates them to constantly encounter academic apathy in their classrooms. And as hard as they try, teachers can't do it all, despite what states and communities demand. Educators today need lots of help from administrators and outside advisers who understand the dynamics of instruction and the frequently irritating behavior of adolescents.

At the freshman academy, the person who usually steps in to meet the need is Scott Peterson. "I wouldn't be here if it wasn't for Mr. Peterson," Zack explained. "I'm in gratitude to him."

Ask many freshman academy students, particularly boys, why they try to overcome perpetual truancy, classroom misdeeds, or academic laziness and "Mr. Peterson" usually is mentioned in their answers. (Girls tend to lean on guidance counselor Mimi Cantrell or other female faculty members.) Students know that, technically, Peterson is not a teacher in his role as the academy's dean, but titles and technicalities aren't particularly relevant to teenagers. Relationships are.

Constantly on the move during the school day, Peterson

pulls one student out of class to discuss behavior issues, tends to another sent to the office for a dress code violation, and comforts a dejected-looking boy by giving him a friendly pat on the shoulder and a "You doin' okay?" Peterson waits for the boy's answer, ready to talk if it's "No."

A burly man with sensitive brown eyes and a round, trustworthy face, Peterson gets in students' personal space, not to intimidate them but to connect. He seems to know instinctively how to strike a balance between being firm and friendly. Perhaps because he's new to the dean of students role or because he's trying so hard not to emulate the punishment-focused assistant principals who are so common in high schools, Peterson makes a conscious effort to view education from the students' side.

"We've just got to improve the quality of student life," he says.

He planned to attend law school after graduating from college twenty years ago, and approached teaching as a fallback job. After completing his student teaching stint, however, he never looked back. Nowadays, like the idealistic public defender he might have become, Peterson tends to treat his underserved students as his clients. He continually fights the system, putting pressure on teachers and administrators at the freshman academy and at Jefferson and Lincoln high schools to consider the teenagers as individuals instead of blindly enforcing rules without discretion. Peterson acknowledges that his actions have earned him detractors who view his vigilance as a nuisance, resent his interference, and accuse him of being biased in favor of students.

"I respect every person in this building professionally," Peterson said, recognizing the occasionally uneasy alliance. "Before the end of the year, I'm going to write a letter to each staff member, saying, 'If I've pissed you off during the year, I'm sorry, but I was looking at the situation from the kid's perspective.' The relationship with the kids is not fifty/fifty in the inner city. It's not about the adults' self-esteem. It's about the kids."

Although he may have critics among the freshman academy teaching staff, Peterson has the full support of many others. English teacher Ellen Jackson said she believes Peterson's critics are guilty of "not buying into what this school is about." She wonders what teachers expect Peterson to do when "all these kids have known for fifteen years is punishment, punishment, punishment."

Science teacher Hynes agrees. "This school is largely about relationships...with students and teachers, and only when you build that can you make a change academically," he said, adding that teachers who complain about Peterson's approach don't have much ground to stand on if they refer their classroom discipline problems to him.

"Here's the deal," Jackson said, summing up her support of Peterson. "You don't have to agree with the administration, but once you turn it over to them, it's your fault. You can always go in and talk to Scott, and you'll get consideration and you'll get respect."

Peterson doesn't dwell on criticisms that come his way. He's too busy targeting policies and practices that he considers detrimental or unfair. For example, he became incensed when the school district adopted the recommendation of a former local FBI chief-turned-school-district-security director that students should pay a $5 fine every time they came to class without their required laminated identification badges. If students didn't have the money for the fine, they were supposed to go home to get it. Not surprisingly, as Jefferson and Lincoln administrators found out, many students left school and did not return.

"You know, you're trying to teach a kid physics, you're already in an adversarial relationship, then you gotta check for their badge and send them home because of that!" Peterson said hotly. With a monetary punishment, he said, the students who don't have the money will just stay home. Rather than enforce a policy that interfered with their efforts to connect with and teach students, Peterson and several freshman academy teachers usually chose to drive the teenagers home so they could get their badges and quickly return to class.

Another time when a freshman academy teacher wanted to punish a group of students who had not pushed their chairs under the tables after class as directed, Peterson suggested that she might explain her reasoning to the students instead of issuing a decree they would consider just another ridiculous institutional rule.

In many other ways, Peterson and some of his colleagues

advocated for students during the school year. Instead of excluding students whose families couldn't afford for them to participate in extracurricular activities, the staff members often paid their fees. One student, accustomed to earning good grades in middle school for low-quality work, became a behavior problem when his freshman academy teachers held him to higher standards of performance. Peterson counseled the boy and helped him see that his teachers didn't blame him or consider him stupid; they wanted him to push himself. By the end of the year, the boy was learning to accept the challenge and earning A's and B's. Peterson noticed that another student's standardized test scores revealed knowledge and skills greater than his low grades would indicate. It turned out that the student had suffered severe emotional abuse at home and was so distrustful of adults that he alienated his teachers so they couldn't get close to him. Hundreds of mentoring hours later, Peterson broke through the student's emotional wall and persuaded him to consider achieving closer to his potential. Another time, after discovering that a student was intentionally misbehaving to earn after-school detentions rather than go home to a parent he feared, Peterson added the boy to his personal triage list.

In terms of parent involvement, "there's no in between," Peterson said. "Either it's good or there's nothing there."

There were many successes at school during the pilot year, but some days there were just "too many fires to put out," he said. Midway through the school year, Peterson worried that he was overextended and emotionally spent. Colleagues shared their concerns that he was taking on too much. In one of the rare moments when he would admit that he sometimes felt defeated, Peterson wondered whether he should leave his administrative post and return to the classroom.

"I think I could have a greater impact on them if I was their teacher than I am in this position, because you have that day-to-day interaction with them," he said. "You know, you're not just seeing them when they're in trouble."

Then, as if all he needed was to express the thought to overcome it, Peterson quickly sat up and changed his tune. "But I'm committed. I'm definitely committed to carrying this thing through until wherever it is we end up," he said.

Most days Peterson had help from his colleagues on staff. Sometimes their collaborative support was so powerful that it literally protected the teenagers from harm. Near the end of the school year, a female student entered the freshman academy office, crying hysterically. She reported that a peer at her home high school had threatened her life and planned to drive by the academy after classes were dismissed and shoot her. Lewis and Peterson quickly notified the faculty of the potential disaster. One teacher stayed in the office to comfort the girl, and the others posted themselves around the school building as students left to board buses, erecting a human fence to protect one of "their kids."

On another occasion, math teacher Gary Rosenberger stepped in to provide critical academic care to students. Lewis had hired the twenty-nine-year veteran of the Gladston school system as the freshman academy's math tutor. The position was designed as a sort of safety net, an extra faculty member to keep students from progressing to more advanced high school math courses without first understanding the basics. He was to pull struggling students out of class and provide them with individual or small-group attention. But because Rosenberger was not assigned to a specific teaching team or group of students, he spent the first semester working in isolation and regretting that he had joined the academy staff. When students received their grades after the second nine-week period, however, Rosenberger not only seized an opportunity to save some students from failure, but also resurrected his belief in the freshman academy's purpose and potential.

He designed a "credit recovery" program targeting students who were in danger of losing their freshman year math credit. (This process later would become one of Chief Education Officer Denise Bannister's major efforts to spread the freshman academy's reforms throughout the Gladston school system.) He persuaded sixteen students to enroll in the program, which required them to stay after school for ninety-minute sessions five evenings a week working both independently and one-on-one with Rosenberger (who volunteered his time) on basic computation exercises and advanced word problems. Participants and their parents had to sign a contract agreeing to specific expectations of behavior, attendance, and outcomes. Six of Rosenberger's initial group dropped out, but the remaining ten stuck with the rigorous program and developed sound math

skills; seven of them passed their regular high school math classes for the year.

Ryan was one who succeeded. The freshman was failing
algebra at Lincoln High School when Rosenberger stepped in
and persuaded Ryan's counselor to move him to a pre-algebra
course so that he could build a better foundation for algebra.
The counselor agreed. Encouraged, Ryan decided to attend
Rosenberger's credit recovery class. Soon after, his outlook on
school soared along with his grades.

"Here [at the freshman academy], they give you second
chances," Ryan said. "If they didn't give us second chances, most
of us probably wouldn't be here now. We'd be in trouble."

All ten students who completed Rosenberger's course did
so with a grade of 90 percent or higher. In addition to the credit recovery course results, those students and others who periodically took advantage of Rosenberger's help at the urging of
their freshman academy teachers posted improved scores on the
state proficiency tests administered in the spring of 2000. The
morning after they received the test results from the state, one
team of teachers and students greeted Rosenberger with a standing ovation and a surprise breakfast.

Rosenberger minimized his role in the program's success
and praised the students instead. A former struggling student
himself, Rosenberger said he told the freshmen he was guiding
that they could pass the proficiency test; they simply needed to
refresh their understanding of basic concepts and remember to
break word problems into manageable steps before trying to

solve them. His experience demonstrates that educators, like the adolescents they teach, need to feel that they belong to their schools.

Teacher Clyde Dalyrymple also did his part to connect to students whom he viewed as needing more positive role models in their lives. For Dalyrymple, the hook was technology. A staunch supporter of integrating computers and related equipment into every subject, he often annoyed his colleagues who were too overloaded with the demands of troubled teenagers and the pressures of proficiency tests to be vigilant about making technology connections in every class. Dalyrmple also could be abrasive with other teachers, which alienated instead of encouraged them to find ways to include him in their team planning.

But he was clearly effective with students. Intent on taking advantage of teenagers' interest in technology, he introduced a wide range of electronic applications, including computerized academic portfolios, multimedia presentations using sound and animation editing, and Web page designs. And he did it with such gusto that even the most apathetic students took notice.

"That's the beauty of virtual reality," Dalyrymple boomed one afternoon as he marched around the technology lab gleefully explaining his latest cyber-fascination to students. "You don't even need to leave the classroom and you can see places you might never visit."

Dalyrymple frequently opened his computer lab after school, including organizing a technology event to showcase students' work for parents and the community. For some students, Dalyrymple's enthusiasm brought special joy to their learning.

"And Mr. Dalyrymple, well it's like every time we go in that class we learn something new," a student named Kristina told an audience of nearly 200 Gladston educators in May 2000 as she explained the benefits of attending the freshman academy. "That's all we do in there is learn."

"I learn the most in technology," a student named Edward said one afternoon in the freshman academy lobby, "because he [Mr. Dalyrymple] talks to you and you learn more…. It's the class I like 'cause I like computers."

During the technology demonstration event that Dalyrymple sponsored, a freshman named Marcus sat at a computer seeking an audience with everyone who passed, eagerly demonstrating his knowledge of Web page design and Internet research. "I just love computers," Marcus said, beaming at his machine. "I want to be a computer programmer when I grow up."

For all their triumphs, the freshman academy faculty was not universally successful. One student who enrolled in the freshman academy was so deeply troubled and involved in gang activities that extensive efforts by his teachers couldn't prevent his home high school from expelling him at the end of the first semester. Although he intervened to help a persistently truant student whose mother needed him to care for his four younger siblings while she worked, Peterson wasn't able to keep the boy from failing his classes. English teacher Ellen Jackson worked diligently with Peterson to help another student — a seventeen-year-old freshman — overcome his academic and social barriers. Despite repeated attempts to make up for the huge void in the boy's home life and prior schooling, Jackson and Peterson couldn't turn him around in time. The four academic credits he earned were not enough to elevate him to sophomore status. Peterson lamented another student who failed every class at the freshman academy — despite the ratio of one adult for every ten teenagers — because his academic skills were weaker than the faculty had the time or the talents to improve.

One student, who had nearly exhausted the patience of his teachers with repeated misbehavior and refusal to complete assignments, offered a surprising suggestion. "They [the academy] should have an after-school class to learn more about college and careers and what you need to do," he said. "Not for credit, but just to learn."

Freshman academy faculty members tried to start several after-hours activities for students, including intramural sports. But they lacked money, volunteers, and space to do everything they wanted. When school district transportation officials wouldn't provide bus service for students at Lincoln to return to the freshman academy in the afternoon to serve detention or to work on computers, Peterson added personal driver to his list of duties until he eventually persuaded officials to relent and provide the transportation.

One of his most successful projects was Sunset School, which he based on a similar program in Baltimore. It was

designed as an alternative to sending students out of the classroom as punishment for bad behavior. Whether students are
made to sit in a school conference room for the remainder of the
day or stay home for three days because of suspensions,
Peterson believes these traditional methods of detention contribute to delinquency. Many students consider out-of-school
suspension "an attractive option," he said, because there are no
adults at home to monitor their behavior. These same students
often are in danger of failing; he wanted to keep them in school
where they might learn. Likewise, he said, the high number of
repeat offenders at in-school suspension programs suggests
some weaknesses in that method of punishment, which typically involves no clearly defined structure or purpose.

During supervised after-school sessions at Sunset School,
students had to write personal reflections about their misbehavior and come up with goals to improve it. They also had to
complete assignments missed because of their outbursts in class
and study for any subjects on the state proficiency tests they had
not yet passed. Peterson agreed with teachers that students needed to experience repercussions when they intentionally broke
school rules, but he argued that only by eliminating lapses in
learning could the staff significantly reduce behavior problems
and provide the support system students were seeking.

As word spread among students that getting sprung from
class was no longer an option, many complained that the alternate plan was unfair. And, as spring approached, ill-behaved students who wanted to enjoy the warm weather accused teachers

of assigning an unreasonable number of Sunset School referrals.

"I asked your teachers to rein you in and get you to focus on academics because that's what we're about here," Peterson told a class one Friday afternoon. "We're not trying to stifle you; we just need to stay focused. And by the way, have a good weekend."

Sunset School wasn't an unqualified success, but it worked for most of Peterson's customers. During the 2000–2001 school year, the school system extended Sunset School to the two high schools and made plans to eventually carry it to the district's middle schools.

Edward was a familiar face during the early days of the freshman academy's Sunset School. A year earlier, he had moved to Gladston from one of the roughest parts of Chicago. His first semester at the freshman academy included several run-ins with teachers and an out-of-school suspension from his home high school for getting involved in a fight he said he "couldn't walk away from." After spending more than a few afternoons at Sunset School, however, Edward's behavior began to improve.

"It helped me get focused," he said, acknowledging that the grandmother he lived with in Gladston during his freshman year was strict and supportive but probably needed a little help caring for a teenaged boy by herself.

By the end of the second semester, Edward was staying after school periodically, but not to serve punishments. Instead, he worked for the school janitor or helped technology teacher Dalyrymple with various projects to earn his required community service hours. And despite being identified as a student at risk of failing, Edward passed his freshman year with two credits to spare.

Perhaps the biggest beneficiary of Sunset School and of Peterson's brand of support was Zack. The midyear move to a different teaching team helped him turn a corner, but on many days, Zack still lapsed into delinquency. One day, after he had been warned that another serious infraction would lead to an out-of-school suspension, Zack broke the rules again. He approached Peterson and frantically pleaded for a Sunset School sentence instead.

"Please don't suspend me," Zack begged his mentor. "I don't want to go home. I want to be at school."

His words resonated deeply with Peterson. Zack's pleading contained the implied message that the staff at the freshman academy had succeeded in showing him that school was where he belonged. He had earned enough credits by the end of the term to advance to the tenth grade. Two weeks before he left the freshman academy, Zack told Peterson that he finally had started enjoying school.

"Well, that's good," Peterson said, laughing. "It took a hundred and seventy-five days, but we got there."

12

THE STUDENTS SPEAK

Seven students entered the cramped room at the Jefferson Learning Center and glanced anxiously at the video camera resting on a tripod. Although they were accustomed to seeing and chatting with visitors in the classrooms of the freshman academy, most of those encounters had been informal; the observers seemed more interested in watching the teachers than the teenagers. This time the lens was focused on them.

It was late January 2000, halfway through the school year, and time to take stock of the status of Gladston's educational experiment — from the students' perspective.

The students relaxed somewhat when they spotted Program Leader Janey Lewis sitting with a half dozen adults crowded into the rectangular room, which is barely wide enough for a conference table most days but which now contained ten chairs arranged in a loose circle. Lewis welcomed the students and motioned them to join her and consultant Judy Hummel in the circle.

During the brief get-acquainted time, the students revealed backgrounds and interests as diverse as their physical characteristics. A small boy with baggy jeans and shaggy hair said he spends four hours a day on his family's two computers and believes that having access to technology helps him with his homework. A tall, statuesque girl who plays three different sports said she likes computers but doesn't have one at home. A quiet boy with a full mustache and a bad case of acne talked about how he had taught himself to play three musical instruments that his mother bought at yard sales.

"I want to be an architect," he announced with a grin.

None of the students in this particular group was an identified scholar. They hadn't earned test scores that would place them in the school district's advanced program. Nor were they the kind of students who make a teacher's life hell. They were just average students who were in the interesting, if somewhat unusual, position of being able to tell adults exactly what they thought of them. Although they were promised anonymity — the tape would not be shown to the teachers until after the students had completed the ninth grade — they took awhile to warm to the task.

When Hummel asked the students to describe their most meaningful learning assignments, half described experiences in their middle school classes. One boy spoke passionately about his eighth-grade history project, which focused on military leaders and their impact on World War II. The magazine he researched, wrote, and designed so inspired him that he couldn't wait to help his sister with hers the following spring. One girl talked about a seventh-grade art project and how proud she felt when her teacher selected her work for exhibition at a city art fair. The teacher's high standards helped this student understand what it means to reach for excellence.

When another student mentioned enjoying a rocketry project at the freshman academy, and two others described their exciting out-of-class field trips to a Native American powwow and the regional science center, Hummel asked them what they had *learned* through those experiences. A simple question, perhaps, but the students couldn't answer it. Their inability to articulate the connection between the activities in their classes and the knowledge they had gained suggested that the freshman academy faculty as a whole had not succeeded in showing students the importance of that relationship.

And yet the teachers seemed to be on the right track. They had involved the students in designing and writing a promotional brochure for Gladston's eighth-graders and in leading tours around the freshman academy. They had persuaded students who complained of having "nothing to do" in Gladston to make a formal presentation to the city council suggesting that the town leaders build a teen center; they later gathered signatures for a petition in support of the plan. They had taught students important life skills, including how to conduct themselves in an audience and how to eat and dress for formal occasions. Those and other efforts were starting to pay off. Asked to evaluate on a scale from one to ten how much they had learned during the first semester at the freshman academy, none of the students awarded a grade lower than seven.

"I give it a nine," one girl said, "because it doesn't seem like it, but from the first day of school till now I've learned a lot."

A boy who settled on a score of eight said, "My grade point average is the same and we're learning harder stuff, so I know I'm learning."

"There's a lot more hands-on experiences and not just reading about it in a book," said a student who thought the term merited "an eight."

Over the course of two days, Lewis and Hummel conducted similar conversations with about three dozen students — a representative group from each teaching team at the freshman academy. That they were genuinely interested in seeking the students' opinions was something of a rarity in the Gladston school system, a point that all the teenagers made even when they found something to criticize.

"Our home high schools would never do this," one girl said. "I think that's why we're complaining about the freshman academy; we know something will be done about it. Here we know somebody will listen."

And listen they did. Lewis, Hummel, and several central office administrators heard opinions about the freshman academy's efforts to integrate different subjects, to provide emotional and academic support for students, and to connect lessons to careers. They heard complaints about inconsistent discipline practices and complicated class schedules. They heard praise for administrators who knew them well and teachers who pushed them to higher levels of achievement.

"At my home high school, if you don't do a good job, you just fail," one boy said. "Here, you keep going until you do quality work."

"When I first came to the freshman academy and there were four teachers in one room, I thought, 'We don't need 'em,'" another student added. "Now they come around and can really help you and answer your questions. They don't do that at Jefferson. At the freshman academy, they know who you are and where you're coming from."

"At the freshman academy, they go deeper into an assignment with you," a third student said. "Some teachers at my home high school, they don't have the patience or the time to go deeper into it."

It was apparent that students also had grown more comfortable speaking the language of education reform. In most cases, they recognized the difference between slipshod and exemplary work. Although they hadn't always reached the goals their teachers had set, they had gained a better understanding of why they sometimes failed.

"I know I've done quality work when I can think of nothing else to say about it," explained a lanky, soft-spoken boy who admitted that he had done little beyond "getting by" in middle school. "I feel good about it. I get congratulated from people all around."

A computer-generated slide show that he and a partner had created to discuss the history and scientific principles of rocket propulsion had proved particularly satisfying, he said with a contented smile. "We reached high up to our standards and got the job done.... I like projects. That's when I work to my full abilities."

Another student said she appreciated having teachers who expected more from her. "They can tell when you're doing quality work," she said. "They'll say, 'Trish, you know you can do a better job.' Or last week, I wasn't feeling well and they said, 'Trish, you need to go home. I can tell you're sick.'"

"Even though some of the rules are outrageous, you learn," one girl said. "I made the honor roll this year for the first time in my life. I think they should make more freshman academies, like the junior academy and the senior academy, just harder for each grade level."

With wisdom beyond his years, one boy told how the freshman academy staff had taught him the difference between being average and being excellent. "They can tell if you just wrote something down just to turn it in," he said. "If you're going to go through life and just turn things in for the sake of it, you're not going to go very far."

Many students said they liked the opportunities they had to work with a group instead of toiling alone.

"It helps when you have other opinions," one student said.

"It kind of opens you up to ideas and options," said another.

A question about what they would do to reinvent school elicited some of the most interesting comments during the focus group conversations.

"When they interview teachers, ask them how they teach and make them show some samples of their work and assignments," one girl suggested. "And do some psychological profiles, because there's some crazy teachers."

Another girl recommended that teachers learn how to "work together better. You ask one teacher something and ask another, and you get different answers. They don't know what they're talking about. They need to be more organized."

One girl said she was tired of "useless things we do like calculating attendance percentages. That's their work. There's no point in our doing it."

Later, during a debriefing session with Lewis, Hummel noted that one group of advanced students had struggled more than any of the others in answering questions about what constituted "quality work." Accustomed to earning easy A's for filling in the blanks on worksheets or memorizing facts for tests, they were stymied by — and somewhat resentful of — the freshman academy's requirement that they use their knowledge of basic skills to solve complex problems and explain their reasoning.

For example, in deconstructing the rocketry project that

had absorbed most of the first semester for one team, these students could speak articulately about how their teachers had carefully integrated concepts from each subject and provide remarkable insights about why some jets had sizzled and some had soared. But in every conversation they had about standards of performance, their remarks always centered on grades.

"I really felt happy about it after I got my grade," one girl said. "It did take stress, but in the end it taught me many things. I do want to get into the technology field, and this will definitely help me."

Another girl said she thought she had done well on her rocketry project, "then I got my grade, and not so good. I accepted it, but I did it over and then I got a good grade."

"I thought I did really good work on the rocketry project, and I learned a lot," one boy said. "But then I got it back and it was an F. I did it over and got a C. I did it over and I got a B. What you feel is quality work and what the teacher thought are two different things."

For students who have grown accustomed to dazzling their teachers, earning approval and figuring out the "system," gaining the symbols of school success often becomes more important than feeding any intrinsic motivation for learning. For students who can't — or won't — play the same game, motivation of any kind is scarce. This dichotomy presents a real challenge for teachers who are trying to design assignments that will appeal to both kinds of students. Yet, at the freshman academy, students of all abilities uniformly described the kinds of activities they find interesting and challenging — those that involve hands-on exploration, variety, and choice.

"Give me something that I can *do*," one girl put it plainly. "When we were getting involved in the rocketry project, if we had just read about people who had launched rockets" and not built them independently, "I wouldn't have learned half as much."

However, she said that aside from the rocketry project her science teacher had resorted to the standard practice of asking students to read the textbook and answer questions at the end of each chapter.

"I want examples. I want experiments," she said emphatically.

Other students said they were frustrated that some teams at the freshman academy seemed heavily engaged in projects and presentations while *their* teachers rarely strayed from traditional assignments such as chapter reviews and book reports that required students to summarize information, not analyze it.

"I'd like to read a book and compare it to a movie," one girl said. "I think that would be more interesting."

Such comments suggested that the freshman academy had succeeded in using higher-level assignments and assessments, but not in every subject and not on every team. One area where students said they consistently received rigorous and interesting instruction was in career exploration. These classes are designed to showcase the various fields that students eventually can choose to pursue through the Jefferson Regional Campus's career academies. According to students at the freshman acade-my, the career teachers emphasized practical applications, diverse topics, and frequent rotations that kept boredom at a minimum.

"I like the engineering class," one boy said. "I got to build a model of a house."

Another boy, who wants to be a microbiologist, said he was thrilled to be able to program a robot using computer tech-nology. A girl said she enjoyed preparing a resume and using it during mock interviews with area businesses.

"It's interesting to me to learn all about diseases and vac-cines," said another student, who said she wants to be a physi-cian. "When I go in that class, I feel at ease and I can compre-hend it."

One girl summed up the feelings of many students when she said, "there's something for everyone" in the career classes. "Even if you're not interested in one, you get to change three or four times a year."

At the conclusion of the focus groups, Lewis and Hummel met with the staff of the freshman academy to share the results. They relayed general information but left concerns about specific team issues for private sessions. They also asked the staff to answer some of the same questions that the students had addressed. In response to a question about how they knew when they had succeeded in designing high-quality work for students, science teacher Leticia Herron said,

"When the smart-aleck kids are not being a pain. That's when I know I've done the right thing."

"With my kids, we've got a project right now, we're doing a debate and I've broken them up into learning stations," said social studies teacher Lawanna Hume. "The kids like to perform and show their peers what they're doing. They get excited and bug you about when they can do their presentations. That's when I think you really have something because you don't have to bug them to stay on task."

Hummel reminded the group that students needed constant reassurance that "they're on the right track," just as the freshman academy teachers wanted to know whether they were moving in the right direction. She suggested that the teachers give students regular assessments of their work, both informal feedback, such as verbal summaries, and formal feedback that might include quiz scores and project evaluations.

English teacher Lynne Valdosta responded by saying that she realized she and her teammates needed to be "clearer about the targets of learning…so everything we do allows them to be more successful in hitting those targets."

Lewis took up the challenge herself, promising the teachers that she would provide more ongoing reviews of their progress in making high achievement a possible goal for all students. And she encouraged them to continue listening to the students for clues about how they could improve instruction.

"Listening to these kids, they can tell us so much about what we can do for them," Lewis said. "As a staff, we need to find ways to work with them. They *will* be partners. They understand better than we give them credit for."

13

A RELUCTANT LEADER

L ars Hennepin's six-foot, four-inch frame towers commandingly above the students in his classroom at the freshman academy, but his youthful energy and boyish grin help him blend in. The physical signs of his students' awkward adolescence — orthodontic appliances, facial blemishes, unruly hair, and gangly, unfinished bodies — are all part of Hennepin's past. He's just bigger now.

Hennepin's personality also fits this age group. He's playful, often seen joking light-heartedly with students in the hallway before class and enjoying the many contradictions in adolescent behavior, such as boys with deepening voices but childlike fears and physically mature girls who still whine like third-graders.

But when class starts, Hennepin's face turns serious as he offers students their daily dose of social studies. He is rarely rattled by students' preferences for playing instead of paying attention. When a few boys acted up during an afternoon discussion, for example, Hennepin quickly diffused the interruption without incident.

"Okay, refocus, please," he said, and the students quieted.

He greeted a later outburst by stopping his lecture and standing still. Again, the students got the message. Noticing a perpetually mischievous student looking across the aisle for a friend to annoy, Hennepin moved to stand near the boy without wavering from the discussion, silently preventing the student's planned attack.

"Lars has great classroom management skills," said Dean of Students Scott Peterson. "He really has such a good rapport with the students. They really respond to him."

As with many teachers who comfortably command their classrooms, Hennepin's skills seem to be instinctive. It helps that he's had plenty of practice. After twelve years teaching at Gladston's Truman Middle School, he understands these urban students, where they come from and how they think. More importantly, he shows them that he's in control. Students rarely spend time offering Hennepin elaborate excuses for missed assignments or inappropriate actions. They know he will confront bad behavior and ambivalent attitudes consistently and directly.

His command of the classroom was evident one day when he discussed a previously proposed Student Congress at the freshman academy. Many students had complained that they needed extracurricular activities and a forum in which to share their grievances, so the administrators and teachers agreed to help them organize a student government. Hennepin was surprised to discover that the students on his team had not volunteered to get involved.

"For a group that has a lot of complaints about the freshman academy I sure didn't get a lot of takers," he admonished them. "If you're going to be able to sit and criticize, you have to be willing to participate."

Hennepin asked for volunteers, but when none came forward he used the situation to teach an ad hoc civics lesson. He explained that democracy depends on responsible citizens who have a voice in government. The students sat obediently through his comments but stared blankly at him. Dismayed but undeterred, Hennepin ended the brief discussion and launched into the day's lesson.

"You're going to learn things today that probably 90 percent of the freshmen in the United States don't know," he told the class, creating anticipation. He asked students if they believed that historical events followed a pattern. While most of them waited for Hennepin to answer his own question, two boys from the back of the room energetically waved their hands.

"Yes!" they called out in unison when Hennepin looked their way.

His smile and theirs expressed emotions wider than a grin. Both boys had given other teachers fits, but they behaved and often participated in Hennepin's class, demonstrating the importance that students place on engaging instruction and personal relationships.

Hennepin spent the next few minutes explaining various theories in history, maintaining order by walking around the classroom and standing near students, sending a silent reminder of who was in charge. After a short break to chat about an upcoming basketball game that had preoccupied his students, Hennepin moved back to the history lesson.

"Okay, let's refocus," he said, issuing his standard call to order. "The next point is going to sound complicated, but just take it easy." As he explained how the German philosopher Hegel described the practice of arriving at the truth by an exchange of logical arguments — stating a thesis, developing a contradictory antithesis, and combining and resolving them into a coherent synthesis — most of the students stared in confusion. It's a complicated concept, particularly for high school students who have spent little time processing deep intellectual ideas, but Hennepin conveyed his belief that they were up to the task.

"It's like an argument," exclaimed an attentive, excited student who suddenly made sense of the theory.

"Vince says it's kind of like an argument, and it kind of is," Hennepin said, smiling and nodding in agreement. "Let me explain how it plays out in history."

After recounting the events that prompted the original thirteen American colonies to revolt against British rule, Hennepin made an analogy that any teenager could understand.

A parent-imposed curfew was a thesis, he said. A teenager's resistance to the curfew could be considered an antithesis. And the compromise that might result from their competing views was a synthesis. Every student nodded in agreement. Many smiled, pleased with themselves for following the train of thought to the end and sensing that Hennepin had somehow elevated their family arguments to high art.

The rest of the class continued in the same way. Hennepin built students' interest in the Marxian theory of dialectical materialism by prefacing it with, "You want to know a big word that you can impress people with?" Minutes later, when students giggled at a rendering of the ship *Titanic* that Hennepin drew on the chalkboard to illustrate social class differences, he comfortably laughed at himself.

"That's probably why I should teach social studies and not art," he said, but then moved immediately back to his explanation of how social class structures can exploit the weak. Students nodded, having seen the movie *Titanic* and the many areas of the ship where only affluent passengers were allowed.

Students left class that afternoon enthused about an arcane topic that others might have considered beyond their intellectual reach. A few students bandied about the idea of running for the Student Congress, bringing Hennepin's social studies lesson back to its original point. It was another clear example of how skillfully the teacher had connected the content to the classroom and to the larger community. Hennepin stitched all the pieces together seamlessly.

But as hard as he worked to model his passion for learning for his students, Hennepin resisted doing so with his peers. During staff meetings, he usually hid his intellectual yearnings behind the antics of the class clown, often to the distraction and annoyance of others. And he frustrated supervisors who saw his obvious leadership skills and wondered why he was so reluctant to use them.

Throughout the first year of the freshman academy, Hennepin fought becoming a full participant on his four-person team, demonstrating through his actions that he didn't fully support the reform. Skeptical of the freshman academy's push for project-based learning, he stated during a faculty meeting that he considered it an educational fad like an ice cream store's flavor of the month. He also said he was frustrated that the freshman academy and other major reform efforts seemed to be driven by corporate backers who have spent none of their adult lives in the classroom.

"Since when is it corporate America's role to tell me what to teach my students?" he asked rhetorically. "Since when is it my responsibility to teach students so that they fit into certain jobs rather than to teach them to appreciate learning and knowledge?"

It's a fair question and one that Hennepin's colleague, fellow social studies teacher Doris Eickmeyer, comfortably rationalized.

"Business and industry have always determined what we teach our children," she said matter-of-factly.

Such an explanation works for Eickmeyer, a self-proclaimed pragmatist. It's a little more difficult for a brooding intellectual like Hennepin. He finds it hard to separate what's truly good in the academy reform model from what's required to satisfy external audiences.

To Program Leader Janey Lewis, disagreements among the faculty about the vision of the freshman academy make it doubly hard to persuade students to engage in lessons that require them to apply their knowledge of multiple topics, not just recall facts for a test.

"As teachers are trying to adapt and change, some of that is rubbing off on kids," she said. "Because frankly, kids would be much more comfortable just to have to read page forty-four and do the obvious questions" at the end of the chapter. "They're experts at doing the class seatwork thing. We've given them eight years of practice in many cases. And I'm not just disparaging what others have done prior to our getting these kids, but that regular kind of class work they've come to know is not what I want to see."

To fulfill those broader ambitions, good teachers such as Lars Hennepin have to become more inclusive, willing to share their skills and spread their influence so their colleagues can grow, too. Moving more students ahead — not just those who come ready to learn — means that schools must fill their classrooms with competent teachers. Individual excellence is no longer enough, for students or their instructors.

Team teaching can be a good way to propel collective

achievement. In addition to helping students see the connections among different subjects and understand how they can use their knowledge to solve problems in multiple settings, a strong team of teachers can build relationships with more students. Different personalities and instructional styles suit some students better than others. Good teams capitalize on that, using a student's affinity for one teacher to build bridges with others.

"Finding that match is really hard," Lewis said, adding that there is no one right way of teaching, for adults or children. "There are different methods of being excellent, and we have plenty of really traditional teachers who are quite excellent and plenty of really innovative ones who are, too. So, it's not just the method."

In addition to improving instruction, schools must establish communities that believe everyone can learn, including from each other. Hennepin acknowledged struggling with this part of the professional practice at the freshman academy. And he's not alone. Educators throughout the country find forced collegiality uncomfortable, at least in part because they have grown up in environments that rewarded their solitary ways.

At the same time, some teachers have been burned by their initial attempts at working on a team. Hennepin recalled that at the middle school level teachers often collaborated on teams, but that the teams did not interact with each other. "It became five schools within a school; my team and my kids," he said, adding that such a setup tends to spread different standards and practices throughout the building.

Hennepin's reluctance to share instructional space with other teachers also had to do with issues of trust. How vulnerable could he be around others? In a city that historically has applauded athleticism over academic achievement, men such as Hennepin are understandably edgy about being identified as intellectuals. He indulges in athletic workouts and bodybuilding not just as a means of over-forty weight-watching but also to avoid looking like the skinny, brainy lightweight of his youth.

Mindful of the awkward stages teenagers go through, Hennepin worked hard at letting his students know they're okay. He regularly joined Peterson's Saturday morning basketball games, during which the two men, along with social studies teacher Trevor Hunter and a few fathers, got good exercise while serving as positive role models for students. During the 1999–2000 school year, Hennepin coached the boys' basketball team at Truman Middle School. But his after-hours work with students on academic projects or with fellow faculty members on integrated curriculum design was limited, despite being a divorced man with no children. Hennepin explained that while he doesn't make space in his life for professional affiliations, he spends a great deal of time at home developing and refining lesson plans. And he routinely expands his subject knowledge through personal reading.

"I put my heart into teaching and the kids," he said emphatically. "I grow angry when I hear teachers talk about how many years they have till retirement."

Hennepin is the type of teacher the freshman academy

wants to cultivate, indeed *needs* to cultivate, if Gladston hopes to raise its high school graduation rates. He knows how to inspire many of his students. But at the freshman academy he also has to show them new ways to demonstrate their learning. And within the academy's collegial framework, he also has the obligation to show other teachers how to improve their practices.

Hennepin didn't always use his leadership ability wisely during the academy's first year, and not surprisingly, his team had only limited success in helping all students learn at high levels. Collectively, the group of teachers failed more students than any other teaching team at the freshman academy. Instead of using his role as the team coordinator to show his colleagues how to improve the consistency and quality of their instruction, Hennepin allowed their personality conflicts with other faculty members and their disagreements about grading and discipline practices to distract them from more important issues.

His team's limited success might have been the kick in the pants he needed because by the time the school year ended, Hennepin had started to believe in the promise of the freshman academy and his own need to change. Through coaching from Lewis and guidance from some of his more senior colleagues, he began redirecting his energies as a lead teacher.

"I see too many teachers doing the same old thing and just falling back. There must be something better," he said. "I'm not sure if it [the academy] has all the answers just yet. It may in the future. But it is the only place I know where there is at least an attempt to make things work. It may not succeed, but...they are trying and I want to give it support. How long until we see results? I have no idea…but it deserves a chance."

14

BUILDING A COMMUNITY
OF LEARNERS

When Janey Lewis walks through the freshman academy each day, she's not just on the lookout for chaotic classrooms or students wandering around the building. She's seeking connections.

"Hey, Sean, how's it going?" she paused to talk with a student on her way up the stairwell. "Got baseball today?"

"Yeah," the student said, looking excited and eager to talk with the principal, or program leader, as Lewis likes to be called. "We'll win. They've got nobody."

"Well, watch that your head doesn't swell too much, buddy," she replied good-naturedly.

For several minutes, the freshman and the administrator debated the relative merits of the two high school baseball teams scheduled to play later that afternoon. Lewis knew all the players' names and their positions.

After her conversation with Sean, she walked into a class-room to observe a course called Freshman Connections, where students learn family and consumer sciences. On this day, they were preparing career folders filled with information about their academic background, job skills, and letters of recommendation. In an adjoining classroom filled with computers, other students from the same team created electronic portfolios, automated resumes that include links to samples of their schoolwork. Students congregated around Lewis, and she asked them questions about the assignment.

Later, on her way up the stairwell to the top floor, Lewis encountered another student who asked her if she had a Bible he could use as a prop for a dramatization in his English class. Lewis already knew that the student's teacher had directed the class to write and perform skits interpreting the play *All My Sons.* This student's job was to assume the role of a preacher delivering a eulogy, and Neel showed him how he could improvise speaking from a podium in a funeral parlor, including raising a fictitious Bible in the air for emphasis.

"Oh, yeah," the student nodded, grateful for the advice. "Thanks. Thanks a lot."

"Thank *you,*" Lewis called after him.

In another classroom, she was concerned to see the lights out and students watching a movie, particularly because the class was being led by a substitute teacher filling in for the regular English teacher on maternity leave. Lewis asked a student to explain the activity. When she learned that the students had first read the book, *The Most Dangerous Game*, and now were watching the movie version to compare the two interpretations, her wrinkled brow relaxed.

After she left that session, Lewis sat in the back of another classroom and observed a social studies lesson in progress. "Lars is working on a project to show them how art and music reflect the culture of the times," she explained on the way out, adding precise details of the way the team of teachers had collaborated on a nine-week project about the nuclear age. Clearly, this was one Gladston School administrator who didn't observe the teachers on her staff just once every five years.

Neel next returned to the English classroom to watch students perform their skits about *All My Sons*. She waited until the first group had finished before asking one of the performers, "Emily, what was your relationship to the deceased, the dead person?"

"I didn't really have a relationship," Emily answered, explaining her characterization. "I was trying to back away because he was my husband."

"Well, that wasn't clear to me," Lewis said in a slightly disapproving tone meant to convey her disappointment that the student had failed to meet her expectations for high-quality work.

Leaving the classroom, she ran into Dean of Students Scott Peterson, who was on his way up the stairs to find her. He reported that a troubled student who had attended the freshman academy that morning had been caught playing hooky from Jefferson High School during the afternoon. The boy and other students were found in an abandoned house near the downtown campus.

"He'll lose his [freshman academy] credits," Lewis said, sighing, when Peterson told her that the student would be suspended for ten days.

After school, Lewis conducted a brief faculty meeting in which she focused on plans for the next day's field trips to area colleges and universities, part of an effort to get all of the freshmen thinking about higher education. Making a quick switch from being an instructional leader to the academy's chief traffic cop, she reminded the teachers that they must help supervise the morning and afternoon school bus transfers.

"Last week we had an incident, a fight," she told them. "I was out of the building and Scott was the only one there. We really need to have someone from every team there. Our presence helps prevent a lot of difficulties."

Before the meeting ended, Lewis said that while only one month remained in the school year, it was not too late for the teachers to improve their relationships with students, including calling home and consulting with parents if necessary.

"I want to say with my head held high that we did all we could to help every kid succeed," she called out.

More than anything else, Lewis' first year as program leader of the freshman academy can be summed up by that statement. Whether navigating the bureaucracy of the school district, negotiating with administrators at the two Gladston high schools, or nudging teachers to strengthen their lessons, Lewis always has students on her mind. She is part cheerleader, part drill sergeant, part curriculum coach, and part surrogate mom, a tireless educator who believes so passionately in her purpose that she doesn't hesitate to trample turf issues that threaten to block her progress.

Lewis has intimate knowledge of every teacher's practices. She also knows all the students in the freshman academy — which ones are having discipline problems, which ones are achieving, and which ones could be doing more.

"Janey is having success because she's never strayed from the focus" of the freshman academy, of helping all ninth-graders make a successful transition to high school, says Judy Hummel, the faculty coach from the Center for Leadership in School Reform. "She's providing the leadership."

An attractive, cheerful woman in her early fifties, Lewis exudes the energy of someone fifteen years her junior. In her jumpers, sweater sets, and loafers, she looks like she's still dressing for high school, although perhaps at a time when the style was not as informal as it is today. Lewis relates well to students, and she's as optimistic and idealistic as any adolescent. But even as she dreams of shooting for the stars, her mind and feet are planted firmly on the ground. Lewis is nobody's fool.

"I don't think people realize just how tough she is," Peterson says about his boss. "She's not afraid to confront issues."

During the course of the year, she challenged teachers who failed to reach her high standards or who failed too many students. She forced staff members to meet with students and hear their side. She alternately praised and prodded people, using whatever exhortation she deemed suitable to get them to produce. Yet, as hard as she pushed the staff and students at the freshman academy, Lewis also made sure they received regular recognition — intercom announcements of key milestones, after-school parties with cake and soft drinks, and celebratory memos sent to her staff of "Don Quixotes." In one of the latter notes she wrote to the teachers in mid-April 2000, Janey "Sancho Panza" Lewis reminded them that "Yes, Don Quixote tilted with windmills and some thought it folly. However, he continued to fight for the ideal despite all obstacles. He saw every person as someone of great value. His life blessed all in its path. So will ours as we continue to press forward with total reform."

Some believe that Lewis' crusade is indeed an impossible dream, from teachers who think students should bend to their whims and not the other way around, and administrators from within the Gladston school system who think Lewis tends to coddle urban punks, to some of the students themselves who can't understand why this big-hearted woman keeps pestering them to achieve.

It's a common occurrence at the freshman academy to see Lewis huddling with a group of students in a classroom or meeting with them in her "office," a simple desk squeezed into a crowded room and surrounded by Peterson's desk on the left side, guidance counselor Mimi Cantrell's desk on the right, and school secretary Kimberly Meredith's desk and a copy machine in front. By design, the space was supposed to be open and accessible, and it is, although it was not intended to be the constantly busy, public gathering space it turned out to be. The lack of privacy in the office can be distracting. On some days, all three administrators at the freshman academy counsel students at their desks, the telephones ring continually, and other students and teachers mill about near the doorway, waiting for a chance to talk.

Peterson acknowledges feeling frustrated by the crowding sometimes, particularly when sensitive conversations can be overheard. "We're on top of each other here," he says. "But one advantage of us being on top of each other, we rarely have fights here [in the freshman academy] because the teachers are everywhere and kids can't get at each other in open spaces. We've only had three fights this whole year. Kids love this space. They always feel like they get attention."

Lewis both respects students and expects them to do well. An incident during the spring semester showed how far she was willing to go to give students a voice and teach them how responsible adults should confront their differences. A group of students, most of them high achievers, had come to Lewis with a list of complaints about Virginia Addison, their Freshman Connections teacher. Rather than become the intermediary, Lewis challenged the students to select two representatives who would represent them in a meeting with her and Anderson to discuss possible solutions.

During the meeting, Lewis explained to Addison (whom she had briefed privately beforehand) that the students were frustrated, not angry, because they couldn't understand the assignments and deadlines in the class.

"Our goal is to get this resolved," said Ashley, one of the two student representatives, as she passed a list of their written concerns across the table.

"No, it's not that easy," Lewis said, laughing. "We're going to go over each item one by one."

The other student, Ammari, explained to Addison that they weren't trying to be obstinate. They were legitimately confused. "We don't get clear directions on projects," she said. "We think we should all be working on the same projects at the same time so we know what's going on."

"So you would be happy if I said, 'Here's your project. Here's what you have to do'?" Anderson asked her. "No choice?"

The two girls thought for a minute, not understanding that Addison had been trying to get them to start thinking for themselves instead of always relying on the teacher for directions.

"Well, see, we have three different things due, and we're not sure how to meet the goals of all of them, and you do," Ammari said.

"The directions were at each [learning] station," Addison said, her voice rising. "But if you were absent or in math [class], you might have missed some of that."

Sensing that Addison was getting edgy, the two girls started to backpedal, acknowledging that "some of this is not your fault." Lewis, who had been observing the discussion quietly, stepped in to help.

"Is that the part that's missing?" she asked them. "You want to know what you're supposed to accomplish?"

Ammari looked relieved: "We don't understand what we're supposed to do."

Addison, who had been restrained up to that point, suddenly cut loose. "What frustrates *me* is when you say you don't know what the project is. We've been working on it for a semester," she said. "Have I ever not helped you when you've asked? I want to make this better, so I'm open to hearing this, but I'm a bit frustrated, too."

The two students shifted some of the blame to their regular academic teachers whom, they said, never seemed to know what Addison was doing even though they sat in during her weekly classes. Lewis said she would talk to the teachers and ask them to better coordinate their work.

"Um, and another thing," Ashley said. "Once we get a handout, we need a detailed explanation of what we're supposed to be doing to complete it."

"So you want an actual form filled out?" Addison asked her pleasantly.

"Yeah," the girls said together.

"Okay, I can do that," she promised.

During the next ten minutes, they discussed several more issues, including a suggestion that they designate one student at the end of each class to be responsible for asking a few questions designed to recap the lesson, then brainstorm answers with the group.

"We need to work together better as a team," Addison acknowledged for her and her colleagues.

"Yes, we do," Lewis said, laughing and looking over at Addison. "They've pretty much nailed it, haven't they?"

Addison, looking visibly more relaxed and conciliatory, turned to the two students. "I'm supposed to be the planner [for the classes] and the other teachers were supposed to be the implementers, but it hasn't turned out that way with some teams," she said. "We need everybody on board. Everybody needs to understand your career choices and how they fit in with other classes. It happens sometimes very effectively, and sometimes not. You can help us get better at it with this kind of discussion."

"Ladies," Lewis said to the two students as she wrapped up the meeting, "I'm very proud of how you handled this discussion. Let me recap and I'll type these up and give them to all the teachers. One, team teachers need to know what's going on in career explorations. Two, Ms. Addison needs to provide completed models of projects to help you understand what the outcome should be. Three, you want to use some round-robin time for recap. Four, students need to brainstorm at the end of class. I also want to thank Ms. Addison for always being so open and looking for ways we can improve things here."

Ashley seemed to sit up taller in her seat as she said, "I think we should stay for coffee and doughnuts now."

"Good try," Lewis told her, laughing, and escorted the two girls out of the room.

Although she was usually upbeat, Lewis' frustrations and fatigue periodically peeked through. Watching one of the teachers during a routine observation, she saw that the students were not engaged, which is supposed to be a critical feature of the freshman academy's instruction. The teacher's poor classroom management skills were readily apparent, and Lewis' face showed the signs of strain that a mother's does when her child embarrasses her in public. It happened again in another class. Lewis watched in anguish as a teacher plodded through an ill-conceived lesson, then, not realizing that the problem was his, lost control first of his students and then of his temper.

Lewis didn't criticize these or other teachers in front of students, although she does jump in to assist from time to time just as a coach might call out plays during a game. For the most part, she deals with teacher performance problems behind the scenes. Yet, Lewis doesn't always do a good job of prioritizing the fires to fight, which can leave her feeling depleted and her staff feeling resentful that she's almost too ubiquitous.

"We've got to stop running to Janey and expect her to solve all of our problems," special education teacher Joan Hughes admonished her colleagues at an end-of-the-year debriefing conducted by Judy Hummel. "I have never been part of a staff where people went so often to the program leader or director as they do here. Guys, we need to grow up and be responsible and professional. I don't know how Janey has survived all year."

Peterson is Lewis' chief assistant in issues of student discipline and teacher instruction. Daily they share experiences, insights, and calamities with each other, and daily they try to keep burnout at bay. One of their recurring conversations concerns the faculty's inconsistent understanding and application of high-quality assignments and high-quality assessments. The two administrators agree that some teachers fail to see that engaging instruction is the key to reducing discipline problems. Peterson focuses on the students affected by these issues, and he credits Lewis with taking the faculty to task when necessary. He relayed a situation in which Lewis spent many hours consulting with a teaching team that was having trouble working together and, consequently, was avoiding integrating their respective subjects.

"She just told them, 'You have got to get better,'" Peterson said. "And they have really worked hard; they've come a long way. She's a great leader."

Lynne Valdosta agrees. An English teacher, she is a member of a team that was struggling early on. Valdosta, who previously worked with Lewis at Lincoln High School, said she respects the program leader even though they often disagree about classroom strategies.

"I love Janey, but Janey and I have gone toe to toe on some issues," Valdosta said, adding that those experiences had made her a better teacher and team player.

Another former Lincoln colleague, Doris Eickmeyer, agreed that Lewis' chirpy personality conceals a formidable inner core.

"Janey's a dear, but she's tough," Eickmeyer said.

Eickmeyer defends Lewis' toughness with instructional issues and Peterson's with discipline.

"When I have had problems with administrators is when they compromise their integrity or when they ask me to change a grade or look the other way," Eickmeyer said. "Janey and Scott never do."

Although they are friends, Lewis is not afraid to challenge Eickmeyer and her team member Ellen Jackson, another long-time colleague, when she disagrees with their classroom practices. For example, Eickmeyer and Jackson were among the teachers Lewis faulted after the first nine-week grading period in October 1999 for giving a high number of failing grades to students. She asked all the teachers to explain the grades and provide samples of the students' work as evidence. She also asked the teachers to develop action plans for the next grading period so failing students would have a chance to repair the damage from the first period. And she demanded that the teachers share accountability for students' success, such as making themselves responsible for exploring alternative teaching methods that might reach all students. Lewis said some of the F's proved to be legitimate, but she wasn't comfortable with others. She believes some teachers awarded failing grades inappropriately, such as giving an F on one assignment to a student who didn't staple his papers together as directed.

Jackson acknowledges that Lewis was right to question the two dozen F's she handed out. "It wasn't my best nine weeks as a teacher," Jackson said, adding that the death of her father took her mind away from the classroom for a while. Near the end of the school year, Jackson was pleased with her students' performance on the writing section of the state proficiency test but disappointed that many of them scored poorly on or failed the reading section.

"I know if a student is in my classroom and tries, that student will leave knowing how to write well," Jackson explained. "But I told Janey, 'I need help teaching reading.'"

Jackson said it was easy for her to approach Lewis for such help because Lewis rewards such admissions of weakness and encourages her teachers to be learners. She fosters an environment in which teachers can work to improve their craft and not feel threatened by saying they all have more to learn.

Social studies teacher Lars Hennepin recalled a conversation he had with Lewis about continuing his education. Hennepin wanted to concentrate his studies in his chosen field so that he might impart some of his passion for the subject to his students, but conventional wisdom in the academic world says a teacher should get a master's degree in education instead.

"I want them [the students] to think this is as important as I do," Hennepin said with a sense of desperation and frustration. "I know I'd make more money if I went back to get my master's, but I talked to Janey because I needed to hear from an idealist. She said I had to follow my heart."

It would be easy to dismiss Lewis as a starry-eyed do-gooder if she didn't get such good results. Freshman academy students passed the state's proficiency tests at higher rates than their peers who attended full-day programs at Jefferson or Lincoln high schools. Before the test results were known, the freshman academy had received so many applications for the 2000–2001 school year that district officials decided to admit as many as 500 students — 150 more than Lewis and her faculty were prepared to handle.

On many occasions throughout the school year, it was the freshman academy that district officials hailed as the jewel of the Jefferson Regional Campus project. The progress was incomplete, but word of mouth and small successes made Gladston's solution to the ninth-grade problem a hit with officials eager to put on a good face for the community, the Davidson family, and any other potential grantors.

By year's end, Lewis and Peterson were showing signs of weariness from all the pressure. Nevertheless, they kept up the same frantic pace as they had in the beginning of the school year, still trying to make a difference in the lives of Gladston's students, still intent on creating a community of learners.

15

TEAM TEACHING

At the beginning of the second semester the freshman academy faculty members met to assess their efforts in learning to teach on teams. Heralded as one of the hallmarks of the ninth-grade center — a "radical departure from typical secondary education," according to a 1999 promotional brochure — the philosophical underpinnings of integrated instruction constantly strained to accommodate the weight of interpersonal tensions.

"I had hoped that we would have four teams operating absolutely smoothly," said Program Leader Janey Lewis. But "different philosophies that were hidden, perhaps, in the [hiring] interview process and personal problems in people's lives are creeping in and have overcome their abilities to really produce and work well."

Dean of Students Scott Peterson said he was concerned that some teams had allowed petty differences to interfere with progress. People gossiped about each other and stabbed each other in the back. He said several teachers, weary of the many changes they confronted, had resorted "to old habits and ended up disrespecting kids in front of their friends." Peterson said such behavior is a traditional power play that teachers use when they feel uncomfortable with students. Fortunately, because academy teachers worked so closely together, colleagues often witnessed these incidents and privately made suggestions for improvement.

Lewis recalled the private, "gut-wrenching" meetings she had with each team in January 2000 in which one teacher asked her colleagues for brutally honest feedback.

"Am I really the b—— that kids think I am?" she asked one of her partners.

The teacher answered truthfully: "Yeah, a lot of times you are."

In another sign of growth, a teacher who had struggled for months to connect with the urban students he thought he knew so well finally broke through his bravado and came to Lewis, pleading, "I don't know what I'm doing. Help me!"

Since then, Lewis said, all four members of that teaching team had started harmonizing in ways that were starting to pay off in better student discipline and learning. Teachers on various teams had seen the light.

"I think we're finally learning to be a team," acknowledged science teacher Leticia Herron. "We're trying to work in concert with each other, to get into each other's classrooms. There was a whole lot of diversity that we had to get through."

"Two heads are better than one," agreed Virginia Addison, one of the academy's two Freshman Connections teachers. "Team teaching doubles our job and divides our grief. When it works and clicks, it's so empowering to me. When it doesn't, I want to keep at it. It's work to make it work."

Teaming is difficult in any profession. It requires placing faith in people, giving up individual preferences, and losing a lot of the instinctive actions and executive decision-making power that accomplished professionals work for years to earn. Teaming frequently fails in every arena, from sports to government to business, so it's no surprise that it was not an overnight success at the freshman academy.

"Participation and collegiality may ultimately improve a school's effectiveness, but they are very difficult to achieve," Robert Evans writes in *The Human Side of School Change*. "They ask of people remarkable sophistication and commitment, a fundamental shift in roles and perspective that is hard for any workforce to develop, especially if it must maintain its traditional functions and master other innovations at the same time…. Chief among the necessary rules and skills are those for resolving conflict, something at which educators, on the whole, lack aptitude and experience…. Many advocates of teacher empowerment and shared governance tend to imagine that creating participatory structures will generate harmonious, trouble-free decision making; they make little provision for preparing people to resolve conflict. Or they believe that what discord does arise can be handled through constructive, non-confrontational methods of bargaining. Both assumptions are false."[1]

Lewis and Peterson said they put a great deal of thought into choosing team members at the freshman academy. Research on successful grouping practices combined with their professional experience told them that by mixing experience levels, pedagogical philosophies, and personality styles they would produce strong teams. In some cases, the recipe worked. In others, it didn't.

One of the freshman academy's strongest teams turned out to include the two newest instructors as well as two veterans of the Gladston school system. The foursome consisting of math teacher DeLora Sims, science teacher Andy Hynes, English teacher Ellen Jackson, and social studies teacher Doris Eickmeyer seemed more comfortable than others at putting aside individual issues to achieve team cohesion. Yet their backgrounds and personalities were as diverse as any group of students in the building.

Perhaps it is not merely personalities that affect team cohesion, but where each personality falls on a continuum. Sims, for example, was a more assertive version of Hynes, and in Jackson, students got a lower-key Eickmeyer. Thus, these four individuals each occupied a position that defined the personality of a whole team.

Sims and Hynes were rookies. Jackson and Eickmeyer together have nearly thirty years of teaching experience. The two seasoned educators have more than tenure and strong subject knowledge; they are street-smart, understanding Gladston's students and the dynamics of the school district. Lewis and Peterson hoped to capitalize on their experience, betting that the two veterans would share their wealth of wisdom with the two novices who, in turn, would offer the veterans a fresh perspective.

Jackson and Eickmeyer had worked together for years at Lincoln High School and had tried interdisciplinary teaching. But without the strong support of administrators, they had achieved only limited success. Previous experience working together may have been an asset, but the two still had to learn how to adapt to the conflicts inherent in almost any group. They overcame those differences because, like Sims and Hynes, they understood that all teams disagree. The trick was not taking the frictions personally. All four teachers realized the destructive power of allowing wounds and unimportant incidents to fester, only to interfere with instruction. Jackson and Eickmeyer said several freshman academy teachers regularly approached them during the year with complaints about colleagues.

"I don't want other people coming to me about their team members," Eickmeyer said in response. "I don't care. Unless it's child abuse, I don't care who said what to whom.

"We disagree *all the time*," she said emphatically, gesturing toward Jackson. "But it's not personal. It's just not."

Lewis recalled an episode early in the school year when the freshman academy's English teachers had asked Jackson, "How can you do what you do with Doris?" Jackson responded that she had learned "to teach my subject through history. I've got to give up some of my territory to work together." Acknowledging her acumen, the other English teachers asked Jackson to serve as the chairwoman of their department.

Just as skillfully, Jackson worked with her team members throughout the year, sharing insights ranging from instructional and disciplinary challenges to the academic progress and personal problems of their students. Indeed, she was one of the freshman academy's strongest advocates of the necessity of making home visits.

"It opens your eyes," she said. "It solidifies what you think happens at home, such as a mother who doesn't care [about a child]."

Jackson's many strengths were a tremendous asset to the team. But learning to use four distinct personalities and teaching styles to their collective advantage wasn't easy for this crew. The four new colleagues moved unevenly and not always smoothly during their first year together. Here are a few examples:

As students changed classes at the freshman academy, they started filling up the school's large science lab. No bell signaled the four-minute period during which students moved from one room to another. Minus that element of structure, adolescents and adults alike seemed slightly confused. Minutes lapsed before everyone settled down.

A slight, well-groomed man entered the room and politely called the class to order.

"You guys, listen up, please," said the teacher, Andy Hynes.

Students continued chattering, flirting, and arguing about who had been the fifth person seated at the table and, therefore, the one who would have to move to comply with the four-person limit. Some students sat alone and fidgeted with backpacks, notebooks, and identification badges.

"You guys, please," Hynes called out in a gentle but slightly annoyed voice.

Students began to pay attention, although Hynes had to reissue his plea nearly every five minutes throughout the class session.

He launched into a discussion of energy, trying to make some connection with his students who seemed to be in perpetual motion. But like many new teachers who are soft-spoken and serious, he seemed confused about how to work in a setting with so few traditions and rules. For such teachers, urban high schools can be a cruel comeuppance. Freshmen in particular often hold on to the adolescent tactics of the middle grades, trying to test teachers at every turn. It can be maddening for the spectators and just plain mean for the target of the tirades.

About fifteen minutes later into the class period, when Hynes finally captured the majority of his students' attention, a faculty member walked into the room and exited the building, breaking the silence and concentration. The students began fidgeting and chatting all over again. Hynes remained calm and continued with his lecture. Moments later, a second teacher crossed the room to use the external door that connects the building to the faculty parking lot. Hynes looked at the door in silent resignation. An observer wondered why the teachers hadn't used the front door and walked around the block. And who would have designed the building to place one of the school's main exit doors in a classroom?

A few minutes later, a third teacher entered the classroom, this time stopping to check something on a computer in the back of the room. A fourth teacher walked in, and the two interlopers began to converse while Hynes struggled to hold the attention of his students. After several minutes, the two faculty members departed through the outside door. Hynes tried to rein in his students once again.

"You guys, please, listen up," he called gently but more firmly than before. His calm expression started to fade. His jaw locked and his forehead creased with tension. The clock on the wall signaled that the class was almost over. Unfortunately, so were the adolescents' attention spans and Hynes ability to make any real progress.

"He has so much to offer," Jackson said of Hynes as she observed him that day in the science lab. "He's very logical and thoughtful about what he says…very introspective. He just needs to be more forceful."

Hynes has solid subject knowledge and an obvious passion for learning, both the result of spending ten years working in remote parts of the world as an environmental researcher. He decided to make a career change and teach the subject he loves, but his mild manner made it difficult for him to reach some students.

"He's a good teacher. He knows a lot about science," a freshman named Ryan said, adding that Hynes' discipline was too lenient early in the school year. "He's starting to get harder. He's starting to toughen up and take control of his class."

Jackson and Eickmeyer tried to persuade Hynes to change his tone with students so he could command their attention. Intellectually Hynes understood this, but it didn't come as naturally to him as it did with Jackson, Eickmeyer, and Sims, who although new to teaching seemed to possess the same instincts about good classroom management.

Like Hynes, Sims is soft-spoken. Fresh out of college, she is younger looking and smaller than many of the teenagers she teaches yet seems to command them in ways that defy her age and professional experience.

"My favorite teacher is Mrs. Sims because she looks small but she doesn't let anybody walk all over her," a freshman named Seth said one afternoon. "And she knows how to, like, assemble the class and get everybody together."

Sims says growing up on the mean streets of Chicago was infinitely tougher than "anything here [in Gladston]." She learned self-preservation skills at an early age and became determined to survive, and later thrive, in spite of her surroundings. The experience gave her the wisdom to choose her words and actions carefully. She's the personification of "walk softly but carry a big stick."

During their daily planning session, the team members discussed the many activities on their "to do" list: preparing students for upcoming proficiency tests, going to students' homes to meet with parents who hadn't responded to repeated letters and phone calls, and figuring out how to help a student who had developed a phobia of school and missed nearly a month of classes, with her mother's approval.

"The team approach allows you to take the time to intervene right away and deal with situations," Eickmeyer explained. "That's a definite plus."

"The students know they can't play one teacher off another," Hynes added.

After talking with two teachers outside their team about other issues, the foursome did their standard check with one another: "Is there anything else we need to discuss?"

There was. Hynes wanted to talk about how to deal with a fellow faculty member who was supposed to be monitoring several students in his science class. Her frequent absences meant the students were not receiving the adapted lesson they needed. True to form, Eickmeyer and Jackson quickly began trying to fix the situation.

"If it were me, it wouldn't be happening because I've been around a long time," Jackson said, with the tone of a mother defending her offspring. "That's why I'm sitting here so frustrated, because Andy shouldn't have to deal with this."

Hynes sat silently and listened as the two women offered a series of suggestions. Finally, Sims, her voice soft and non-threatening, steered the conversation back to Hynes.

"Why don't we ask Andy what he wants?" she asked gently.

Jackson got the point right away. "You go, girl," she said, playfully slapping Sims on the leg and laughing. "Here Doris and I were automatically trying to solve the problem."

Jackson and Eickmeyer laughed at themselves. Comfortable now, Hynes smiled and then told them what he thought he should do and how he'd like them to help. Problem solved. Nothing personal, Eickmeyer would say.

"Chop, chop, chop. Come on, let's move," Eickmeyer called to her students as they slovenly and aimlessly wandered through the freshman academy's crowded hallway and reluctantly followed her directions to move up two flights of stairs and report to their assigned English and social studies classrooms.

"Chop, chop. Let's go," Eickmeyer called again, and students began to march to her order.

"What's wrong, honey?" Eickmeyer asked a girl who stood pouting and slouching against a table in the hallway.

"I'm mad," the student responded, brows tightly furrowed

and gaze fixed toward the floor.

"You're mad, huh? Well, first of all, you're not mad," Eickmeyer corrected her. "Dogs are mad. People are angry. Get it? Now, what's wrong?" she asked moving close to the student and gently hugging her.

After a brief conversation about the girl's concern that "school is boring," Eickmeyer prompted a smile from her and the two strode into the social studies classroom.

"Okay, let's get started," Eickmeyer called out in her typically loud, commanding voice. "I still see book bags out. Let's get them against the wall."

Students scrambled to the task as Eickmeyer quickly surveyed the students in her charge.

"You're over there, Cierra," she said ushering a young girl out the door and toward another classroom. "Harry, you're in here," she called to a boy still standing in the hallway.

"La Keesha," she called firmly to another loitering student.

"Okay, I'm going," the girl said, knowing her teacher meant business.

Eickmeyer always means business, and although all students may not like it, they know she is consistently firm, and she gets them to perform because of it.

"I like Ms. Eickmeyer, but I just wish she didn't talk so loud," Seth explained one day during lunch. Seth is a high-achieving student, but one who is self-conscious about the negative attention that his aptitude often prompts from classmates. He likes to move quietly through the school day, doing his thing, which mostly means earning A's. That kind of behavior isn't sufficient for Eickmeyer.

"Seth's a good student," she explained. "But he's not completely there yet. He needs to improve his writing."

Eickmeyer has high expectations for every student, and she tries to move them from wherever they start in her class. She challenged Seth to grow in areas where she believed other teachers had let him coast. Setting greater goals for students is part of what defines Eickmeyer as a teacher. Whether she's lecturing in the classroom, shepherding students from room to room, or advising an adolescent in the school office at lunchtime, she is always teaching.

"I just get so excited when I see things grow," Eickmeyer said one day, trying to explain her enthusiasm. "Even if it's just a rose blooming in my garden in the spring, I have to make my husband come out and see it and agree with me that it's *so cool.*"

Eickmeyer says this passionately, as she does almost everything, her inner enthusiasm turning her outer complexion three shades deeper and her eyebrows leaping into a steep arch so that they almost connect to her flamboyant blonde hairdo.

"I don't understand parents who don't want [the best] for their kids," she says. "I want the same for my students as I want for my own kids. And I've never understood administrators expecting more from their own children than they expect from their students. It's unacceptable."

In late spring, Eickmeyer met with a student to explain a low grade she had assigned to his paper. It was another case of a student who had grown accustomed to receiving A's for minimal effort until he was placed in Eickmeyer's class.

"You know I'm going to make you do this over, don't you," she said seriously but without any hint of a threat.

The boy nodded, eyes focused on the table. After several minutes of explaining why she didn't accept the paper he turned in as his best work, Eickmeyer could see she wasn't connecting with the sheepish, somber-looking boy.

"The bottom line is this, Jonas," she said, leaning in so that the faces of teacher and student were only inches apart. Jonas sat up attentively. "Can you do a better job with this? I *know* you can do a better job with this," Eickmeyer said, emphasizing key words. "Do you see that I'm not picking on you? Do you see that I *want* you to be a better writer and to do better? You have a good vocabulary. *Use* it."

Jonas, who had sat sullenly during the session, suddenly laughed. He acknowledged to Eickmeyer that she had a point. He was busted, as students would say. Jonas left the meeting smiling and agreed to rewrite his paper, this time with effort.

"If he thinks he can get away with that, he will," Eickmeyer explained afterward.

Jonas, like most students, wants to be challenged. He liked knowing that Eickmeyer would expect more of him and help him achieve it. Peter Scales, a senior fellow with the Minneapolis-based Search Institute, has conducted and analyzed many studies on the sources of student success and found that the two critical ingredients cited by sixth- through twelfth-graders nationwide are challenge and care.

"The teacher-student relationship is the most central to learning in school and it...needs to be a blend of nurturing and challenge," Scales wrote in a 1999 article in *Middle Ground* magazine. "Students need to believe that their teachers know and value them. But that isn't enough. Teachers need to be like parents — the best ones are both warm and demanding. And for many students, the proof of the caring lies in their exacting nature. If teachers don't expect the best, the feeling goes, then they must not care for me."[2]

Jackson's teaching style is less forceful than Eickmeyer's, but because she understands the essence of the teacher-student relationships Scales describes, she commands equal attention, respect, and performance from her students. A solid instructor, capable classroom manager, willing team player, and dedicated advocate of the freshman academy reform model, Jackson spends as much time as necessary during and after school working with students on assignments. She's modest about her abilities, though they are obvious to her students, who easily relate to her, and to her colleagues, who readily applaud her commitment to teaching and students.

"Ellen is for kids," Scott Peterson said approvingly. "When it comes to someone here who is really *for kids*, she's the best. Bar none."

"I like the academy because you're in the trenches," Jackson said, explaining that it's sort of a haven for educators who care about students.

Jackson said that many teachers "who are really for the kids" don't move into more authoritative roles in the school system because they choose to focus on students instead of their own political safety.

Classroom management is a case in point. To an outsider, disciplinary issues at Jefferson and Lincoln high schools are treated with the same rigidity as turning in homework: you miss assignments, you get a failing grade; you misbehave, you go to the office for your punishment. For every action there's an equal and opposite reaction. The problem with this approach is that the issues that determine why a student misbehaves are often so complex that a standard response is more likely to cause shutdown than compliance. Janey Lewis and Peterson, the two freshman academy administrators, understand that, and they hold teachers accountable for getting to the heart of what causes their students' academic performance *and behavior*.

"They say, 'That's not my job. That's an attendance officer's job,'" Lewis said of many of her teachers who last year resisted making home visits to find truant students or talk to parents. "I say, 'They're your kids. You have eighty fewer kids than a regular high school teacher. You make the calls.'"

Jackson appreciates Lewis' attitude and Peterson's common practice of encouraging teachers to manage students instead of automatically sending disruptive teens to them for discipline. She said it frustrates her to hear colleagues blame high discipline incidents and low grades on students or other teachers.

"That's not right," she said emphatically. "I look at

myself" to blame. "I know I can do a better job, and I *will* do a better job."

The Sims-Hynes-Jackson-Eickmeyer foursome ended the first year of the freshman academy on a high note. Of the four academy teams, they had the highest percentage of students who passed the state proficiency tests and the lowest percentage of students who were sent to Peterson for disciplinary action. On the downside, seven of their students failed to proceed to the sophomore level, and the team never succeeded in getting the student with school phobia to come back to the classroom. On balance, they were pleased, if a little tired, and already talking about the planning sessions they would have during the summer.

PART III

Changing a System

16

LEADERSHIP FROM THE OUTSIDE

By 1999, the powers behind the Jefferson Regional Campus project had decided that they needed a new person to lead the initiative. Nolan Stevens, the former Gladston superintendent who had coordinated the project from its inception two years earlier, wanted to return to retirement. Lyndon LaGrange, the current superintendent who acknowledged lacking the skills to direct a major school reform undertaking, knew he couldn't lead a project that aimed to change a system he had helped to build. And Angelo Hancock, principal of Jefferson High School, said he recognized that his responsibilities would be limited to the high school he already supervised instead of extended to the larger restructuring initiative.

In January, LaGrange and Stevens recommended that the Gladston Board of Education fill the post of chief education officer to serve as both the principal of Jefferson High School and the leader of the Jefferson Regional Campus project. With input from the Davidson Foundation and the Gladston education partnership, the school board decided to establish a position that would operate like an endowed chair at a university with private funds supplementing the public salary. The board hired an executive recruiting firm to conduct a national search and ultimately approved the firm's recommendation to pay the new director an annual salary of up to $130,000 — double the range of $60,000 to $70,000 paid to high school principals in the Gladston school system.

After culling through 170 applications, the school board eventually hired Denise Bannister, a fifty-five-year-old administrator with a doctorate in education and experience as a high school teacher, a district superintendent, a college professor, and the president of a charter high school offering university diploma programs. Bannister assumed her new duties in Gladston only days before the freshman academy and the business academy opened in August 1999.

Although she appeared cautious and deferential during her initial public appearances, Bannister quickly took control of the Jefferson Regional Campus project and eventually assumed full responsibility for restructuring the school district. A sturdy six feet tall, Bannister not only could look her boss, LaGrange, in the eye, she could stare him and anyone else down if necessary. Her soft, almost whispery voice belied her steel-toed approach with staff members and outsiders who challenged her. Within her first six months on the job, Bannister had fired the local advertising firm that the Gladston school system had hired to promote the Jefferson project, fired the out-of-state consulting firm that had begun researching the results of the reform initiative, hired her own communications and marketing specialist, and assumed the new job title of deputy superintendent in charge of school restructuring while retaining the title of chief education officer of the Jefferson Regional Campus project. She also alienated many educators by publicly doubting the rigor of Advanced Placement courses at the two high schools because so few Gladston students took and passed the postsecondary credit tests administered by the College Board. And in March 2000 she decreed that all freshman academy students would begin studying algebra the following school year — all ninth-graders throughout the system within two years — saying existing courses such as "math essentials" and "practical math" would not prepare them for the state's proficiency tests or help them gain access to college. Brushing off concerns that students with limited math preparation would have difficulty succeeding in an algebra course, Bannister said, "It's been done other places." She promised more staff development and computer-generated instruction that would help the students and teachers fill in the gaps.

"Very often in urban school districts," she said during an interview, "people work very hard but they're not really sure that collectively what they're doing is going to pay off to make a difference. There's this notion that all students can learn. If we say that and then go ahead and create all kind of low-level [academic] tracks, we're really making sure students don't learn. So we have to watch what we say versus what we practice."

Bannister almost always had a small mountain of research to back up any claim she made or any shift in direction she advocated. Her lengthy reports to the school system and to foundations were painstakingly documented, almost top-heavy with citations. Her recommendations could be independently confirmed as well. For example, a national study of the effect of taking algebra in high school supported Bannister's view that all Gladston students should take the course, though not necessarily by the ninth grade. The study by researchers at the University of Wisconsin-Madison revealed that students performed much better on a nationally standardized tests when they had completed an algebra course. "These findings indicate that general-math classes should be eliminated because those are low-level classes that lack a strong pathway to the future," said Adam Gamoran, who conducted the study with Eileen C. Hannigan. He added that students with poor math training tend to benefit less from the course than students with more advanced skills, "but they still benefit more than those not taking algebra."[1]

But even though Bannister's analysis was on target, the practicalities of her plans often proved difficult to impart. Many people thought she was right on content but wrong on style; they claimed she didn't spend enough time building bridges within the school system and between the district and its various partners in the community. At least initially, some teachers said, she also didn't fulfill her pledge to provide adequate professional training, equipment, and resources for the staff members who were charged with carrying out her ideas.

Bannister said the right things, such as stressing the importance of collaboration: "If you're going to have a change process, you have to let people develop the change." Yet educators said she continued dictating policies from the top. Her time line was so intense and her manner could be so brusque that she grated on Gladston's polite sensibilities. Eight months into Bannister's tenure, LaGrange, who publicly praised and promoted her, privately asked various community leaders what he should include in her performance review and whether he should terminate her four-year, $125,000-a-year contract because of recurring complaints from educators. In the end, LaGrange not only didn't fire Bannister but also deferred a greater number of decisions to her than ever before.

He explained in an interview that his "thought process had changed considerably" about the importance of school reform in Gladston and his own role in shaping it. Instead of trying to both create and implement the changes, LaGrange said he had reorganized the administration so Bannister would be in charge of design, Deputy Superintendent Herb Mitchell would handle the daily operations of the school system, and he would concentrate on helping the community understand the process.

Asked whether he was the right person to lead the school district through a major reform, LaGrange responded that "only history will tell. My immediate personal response would be no," adding that he would do "whatever is best for the project," whether that meant stepping down or staying on the job.

Some Gladston educators, particularly those who fondly recalled LaGrange's leadership when he was principal of Lincoln High School, resented his decision to position himself as a mediator who no longer actively fought for their interests. For her part, Bannister praised LaGrange for giving her "full authority to do what I need to get done." She said experience had taught her that a superintendent usually has a difficult time leading education reform initiatives because he or she must be an ambassador for so many other issues. "You have to stay above the fray," she said, "and he can't get out there and mix it up."

Bannister, on the other hand, was not afraid to generate tension. A heavy smoker who drove around the downtown campus several times a day to remain in compliance with the school district's prohibition against lighting up on district property, she approached her job in Gladston with an outsider's sense of urgency and an insider's sense of paranoia. She carefully controlled announcements and access to staff meetings, once going so far as to eject a reporter from a December 1999 retreat for the Jefferson Regional Campus coordinators. Although the reporter had been asked to attend as part of her responsibility for documenting the Gladston reform project, Bannister refused to admit her.

"You're not documenting *this*," she declared angrily, then demanded, "Who invited you?"

Informed that Martin Diego, executive director of the Gladston education partnership, had issued the invitation, Bannister interrupted the reporter from continuing. "Well, he had no right to do that," she said. "This is my meeting, and I am the invitee."

When the reporter said she would like to wait for clarification because Diego had not yet arrived at the meeting, Bannister dictated her own terms. "That's irrelevant," she said. "I'm telling you to leave *now*."

At that meeting, and a few weeks later during separate sessions with faculty members from Jefferson and Lincoln high schools, Bannister outlined her plan to expand the Jefferson Regional Campus project. Instead of only rebuilding Jefferson High School through the freshman academy and the four career academies, Bannister said she wanted to use the project as a catalyst to change the entire school system. She defended her actions, saying that the city's two high schools collectively had lost about 1,000 students to private schools in recent years. If the recommended instructional practices and professional development opportunities were restricted to the Jefferson campus, she said, the improvements at Jefferson would not be sustainable and the rest of the district would remain second-rate.

"Building such a community at the expense of other schools within the district does little to improve the overall effectiveness of the district," Bannister said. "In the long run, it will at best sustain districtwide mediocrity."

LaGrange echoed her sentiments. "If it works, you have to

give it to everyone," he said.

Bannister's pronouncement seemed to carry greater weight when the state downgraded the Gladston school district from "academic watch" to "academic emergency," the lowest category in the state's testing and accountability system. "There's no lower to go," Bannister said, and she pledged to put the school system in the "effective" category within four years. In the spring of 2000, she proudly noted that her plan to offer incentives such as free prom tickets to encourage high school students to take the proficiency exams more seriously had prompted higher test scores at both Lincoln and Jefferson.

"Since we have a one hundred thirty million-dollar budget, and this whole thing cost five thousand, it certainly sounds like it was worth it to me," Bannister said.

She correctly surmised that the success of the Jefferson Regional Campus project would be short-lived if its recommended practices didn't spread to other schools in Gladston, particularly to Lincoln High School and to those educators at Jefferson High School who were not currently involved in developing the freshman and career academies. Gladston students would never achieve higher levels of learning if academic standards and classroom instruction were inconsistent throughout the district. And many people appreciated Bannister's public declaration that Jefferson was not the only subpar school in the community. But what really irked those who might have welcomed her refreshing candor was her decision to shift attention from the Jefferson Regional Campus pilot programs before they had received adequate time to refine their practices.

At the start of the second semester of the 1999–2000 school year, LaGrange and Bannister created something of a public relations uproar by announcing that they were extending the Jefferson Regional Campus initiatives to Lincoln. There would be a single comprehensive curriculum in Gladston, they said, with responsibility and resources allocated to the two high schools. They explained the shift in direction to both faculties, but made the mistake of telling the teachers at Lincoln first, which reinforced the long-standing feelings of inferiority at Jefferson. Moreover, Bannister stated that through the reform process Jefferson would cease to exist as an independent institution. She made no such claim about Lincoln, but instead said it would continue to offer the majority of the Advanced Placement courses at the secondary level.

To those who had started believing that the $10 million grant would enable Jefferson to regain some of its past glory, Bannister's comments struck them as a cynical slap in the face. In January, Jefferson Principal Angelo Hancock successfully averted a planned protest walkout by students whose emotions were charged by some of their disenchanted teachers.

"What's happened since Denise Bannister has come on board is that the focus has changed away from Jefferson," said Robert Elkan, toward the end of the 1999–2000 school year. Elkan is a veteran teacher who served on the planning committee for the business academy and now works as Jefferson High School's proficiency test coordinator. "This community, including the board of education, will never allow Jefferson to have any kind of advantage over Lincoln. It just will not be allowed to happen. And right now people here at Jefferson feel that's happened to us again.... There's no trust. And I go back and forth. One day I'll come out of a meeting and I'll think, 'Well, I think it's going to be okay.' And I'll tell people that, then a couple of days later it's all back to the way it used to be."

Diego, too, expressed his frustration with Bannister's decisions. "The grant was for the reconstruction of Jefferson High School to make it a world-class high school. It didn't say *two* world-class high schools," he said. "If everything is going to be dictated by what the rest of the district does, the pilot will never get a fair trial. They say they want to impart what they've learned to the other schools, but they're ignoring the lessons learned so far. They aren't far enough along to know what's working" because of only partial implementation of the recommended practices at the freshman academy and the business academy. "They have precious little evidence to show that the students who weren't achieving are now doing so. So what's the basis for expanding?"

Bannister stuck to her guns. She dismissed grumbling from educators and interested parties from the community as "white noise" that was not distracting her from her goals. "It's all part of what happens, and yes, you expect it," said the former high school social studies teacher. "My experience is that high school teachers grumble no matter what.... I know that's what comes with making change.... You shouldn't take leadership jobs if noise bothers you."

At times, however, she seemed to want it both ways. For example, she said that those who planned the career academies had not spent enough time assessing the students' skills to know what kind of supports they would need to succeed. They had built the programs first, she said, instead of "back-mapping" from the students' skills to the curriculum. Although the freshman academy advertised that students could earn five and a half credits at the academy — a minimum of five credits was necessary to earn sophomore status — some of the students who enrolled the first year could not keep up with the course load.

Nevertheless, Bannister prevented the freshman academy staff members from significantly improving their practices by forcing them to accept 500 students during the second year of the program. With about 170 additional students than its pilot year, far more than the program was capable of handling efficiently or effectively, the faculty had even less time to provide individual attention and avoid future trouble spots. Ten new teachers had to be trained for the 2000–2001 school year, and with the addition of only one new counselor, the administrative staff was stretched almost to the breaking point. Bannister originally expected that the additional enrollment could be accommodated by expanding the freshman academy to the second floor of the business academy across the street. However, she eventually required two teams of teachers and students from the freshman academy to move to a more distant building on the other edge of the Jefferson campus where the crowded classrooms had no telephones, computers, or access to clerical staff.

"The facility doesn't match the work we're expecting kids to do," Dean of Students Scott Peterson said in frustration.

Bannister agreed, calling the facilities issue "the most difficult" one she confronted. The freshman academy wasn't part of the original design of the Jefferson Regional Campus, she said, which meant "we not only had to put it somewhere but find funding for it." But she defended her decision to expand the freshman academy and export its best practices, saying it would be unjust to limit the opportunities to some Gladston high school students instead of trying to reach them all.

"Reports this summer for last school year [1999–2000] showed that the freshman academy on a number of variables did very well and the two high schools did not," she said in an interview in the fall of 2000. "Last week, when we looked at the data for this school year, we're still seeing those huge differences, which says we have to do staff development in all locations."

During her first year in charge of the Jefferson Regional Campus project, Bannister clashed frequently with the freshman academy's Program Leader Janey Lewis. As hard as Bannister was pushing to extend the academy's practices to other schools in Gladston, Lewis pushed just as hard to refine those practices before having to limit the freshman academy's progress for the entire school system's gain. A disagreeable duet ensued in which both women, strong-willed and impatient, fought for their mutually dependent aims. The freshman academy offered Bannister the only quantifiable success from the Jefferson

Regional Campus project that she could report to the community, and the chief education officer controlled the access to money and training that Lewis required for the freshman academy. Like it or not, they needed each other.

"I think the freshman academy is looking very well. I think long term, it will do exactly what it's designed to do," Bannister said. "The problem is that...the faculty folks in both high schools, they see it as separate from them, which is in my view, a potential for failure."

Bannister wanted the freshman academy to be a full-day program which, she said, was in line with the original recommendation from the teacher's union back in 1996. However, others feared that immature freshmen who did not spend some time in their home high schools would simply become immature sophomores who would need help making the transition to the tenth grade. When Bannister asked all of Gladston's high school faculty members to vote on the matter in May 2000, they overwhelmingly chose the half-day program, which also was what the freshman academy faculty publicly endorsed.

At the same meeting in which they rejected the all-day format, the high school teachers also listened to presentations from the freshman academy staff about the lessons learned from the pilot year and plans for the future. Before the meeting, teachers at Jefferson and Lincoln were asked to share their questions or concerns through open-ended surveys distributed by Lewis. Only about a dozen teachers took advantage of the opportunity, but their comments revealed a great deal of confusion about, disagreement with, and hostility toward, the freshman academy's practices.

"How can we communicate behavior problems, responsibility, work problems back to the academy teachers who as I understand it are supposed to be helping these students develop skills needed to be successful at high school?" an unidentified Lincoln teacher wrote. "I have not seen this transformation in a *majority* of the academy students I have."

Other teachers said they thought the freshman academy staff had "spoon-fed" students instead of being tough and consistent about discipline. They questioned whether the emphasis on project-based learning and interdisciplinary instruction was "right" for every student.

"It concerns me that teachers are required to submit a plan for students who have failed, detailing what the teacher will do to ensure that that particular student will pass the next time. How does this prepare a student for the 'real world'?" asked another Lincoln teacher. "Shouldn't the responsibility be placed ultimately on the *student*, not the teacher? It concerns me that the 'philosophy of education' that is followed at the academy will undoubtedly be forced upon *all* freshmen. Is there any proof which [*sic*] supports the effectiveness of the academy for all students? It seems to me that the academy, with its endless supply of chances, would be more beneficial to lower-level students than higher level. . . . Lastly, it concerns me that although you ask for my input it really breaks down to the simple fact that my opinion doesn't matter. What the freshman academy wants, the freshman academy will undoubtedly get!"

Other teachers questioned Bannister's decision to make algebra mandatory for all freshman academy students and to require both high schools to use block scheduling, which lengthens the typical daily class period but alters its frequency during the week. From the comments, it was evident that some teachers resisted and resented the changes both philosophically and practically.

Bannister made no mention of the tensions at the secondary level when she issued a report to the community in the summer of 2000. In it she outlined her plans for the "transition years" up to the 2004-2005 school year, when a rigorous new comprehensive high school program for all students is supposed to be in place at both Jefferson and Lincoln high schools. The planned changes include "smaller learning communities with personalized strategies," a longer school day, a common behavioral management program modeled on the freshman academy approach, and greater use of technology, specifically a computer in every classroom at both high schools.

"The transition process from 2000–2001 will be focused, measured, and collegial," Bannister wrote. "It is important to note that a confluence of variables will need to come together so that rigor for all is successfully accomplished. Continued dialogue for instructional planning and focused resources will be necessary."

Bannister acknowledged having a "rather long series of battles with Janey" about the need to involve more high school teachers and administrators in the freshman academy's training. She said she was particularly concerned that any gains the ninth-graders made because of the freshman academy's practices would be lost if the school district couldn't guarantee that those same students would find similar instruction and emotional supports at their home high schools, Jefferson and Lincoln.

But some educators were skeptical that Bannister's plans would help more in the long run than they might hurt in the short term. Lewis, in particular, became agitated when Bannister decided to open only the arts and communications academy for the 2000–2001 school year, giving the two remaining academies — engineering, industrial, and scientific technology and health, human, and public services — more time to plan. At an August 1999 press conference, Bannister had declared that "three more academies will be open next fall." The changing schedule concerned Lewis because she felt as if she and other planners had unintentionally deceived students who entered the freshman academy during the pilot year by promising them they could move to one of the four career academies as sophomores.

While Bannister and Lewis kept sparring over the best way to build on the freshman academy's successes, research released in the summer of 2000 suggested that the new ninth-grade center was definitely on the right track. Although acknowledging that it wasn't possible to determine which "of the design features of the freshman academy" had contributed to the gains, Bannister wrote in a report to the community, its students had demonstrated "statistically significant differences" in attendance, achievement, and behavior from other Gladston ninth-graders.

"Most notably, 94 percent of the freshman academy students completed five or more [course] credits," she wrote in a report. "If that trend continues, it is likely that 94 percent of the freshman academy students will graduate, as compared against the 1998 high school graduation rate of 65 percent." Moreover, the passing rates were identical for students whether they attended Jefferson or Lincoln. In the report, Bannister promised that the school district would track the freshman academy students to see if those passing rates did indeed hold through their senior year in high school.

According to the research, 94 percent of the freshman academy students earned all the possible course credits, compared with 54 percent of all Gladton ninth-graders in the 1999–2000 school year. In addition, only 8 percent of the freshman academy students had less than a D average, compared with 33 percent of all ninth-graders in the district.

Bannister promised in the same report that "the results of the study will be used to inform practice and to spread the results to all students who attend both high schools." Among the responses cited for the 2000–2001 school year: staff training showing educators how to teach reading in all subject areas; a plan to improve attendance; and time before, during, and after school for students to make up courses they had previously failed.

To improve the connection between high school and college, Bannister arranged for twelve students who were enrolled in Advanced Placement English and six students taking Advanced Placement calculus at Jefferson High School to receive three hours of credit for each course at Monument State College of Technology. She also used the Davidson Foundation grant to pay the college tuition — $89 per credit hour — for the students. Although Bannister said such dual credit programs operated in every other state where she previously worked, the Gladston initiative was believed to be the first in the state.

In the summer of 2000, the Gladston school district — largely through Bannister's efforts — received a matching grant from the United States Department of Education that will supply up to $5 million over several years to establish a college scholarship fund for Gladston middle school students considered at risk of failure. Under the Gaining Awareness and Readiness for Undergraduate Programs (GEAR Up) grant, which will provide tutoring and mentoring, the students will earn a $100 scholarship for every one of the state's proficiency exams they pass, up to $1,500. Pine State University, the Gladston education partnership, and the local YMCA agreed to join other donors in the community in matching the grant through financial and in-kind contributions. In a little more than a year in Gladston, Bannister and her assistants had successfully secured a total of $9.43 million in competitive state and federal grants — including the GEAR Up funds — which Bannister said would be devoted as much as possible to staff development.

Whether Bannister reaches her lofty goals in Gladston remains to be seen. Will Davidson is among those who believe she will succeed. From his vantage point, as the chief benefactor of the Jefferson Regional Campus project and as a member of the Gladston education partnership board, Davidson said many of the conflicts that have surfaced so far in the restructuring project were not unexpected given the difficult nature of educational change. Bannister's insistence on immediate changes might have offended some people, he said, but she spoke the truth about the need to upend the entire Gladston school system. Davidson said he doesn't believe Gladston insiders could ever have fulfilled the mission of the project without guidance from experienced outsiders such as Bannister. Significant reform requires painful sacrifices and new ways of thinking, tensions that the Davidson Corporation experienced firsthand as it reconfigured its factories in response to global competition in the last two decades. Educators generally have a harder time thinking outside the traditions that have hamstrung their profession for almost a century, Davidson said.

"I asked Lyndon [LaGrange] the other day, I said, 'Think about your vision [of reform] when I first talked about it. It was full of clichés, really not confident, really meaningless stuff — 'We will make sure that every child has a good education.' Okay, define that. Every child? So, you're not going to have any dropouts, right? 'Well, about ninety percent [graduation rate],' he says. If you analyzed each of those statements in the original, it was quite a long vision" that was not backed up with specifics.

By contrast, he said, Bannister is trying to deliver the details.

"I think we're heading in the right direction," Davidson said, "but there's a long way to go."

Davidson is right about the difficulty of implementing broad-based change initiatives and about the backlash commonly heaped on those who dare to suggest that the community's schools are not as good as they should be. Bannister might have encountered controversy in Gladston, but she also inherited a system that had stifled its underlying tensions for years, pushing problems below the surface but rarely solving them. She was the bearer of the bad news, not the cause of it.

Unfortunately, observations and interviews suggest that neither a critical mass of educators nor the general population understands what it takes to restructure the community's public schools. Both groups need clear and consistent information about the purpose, the vision, and the sacrifices needed to make education reform work. Such communications do not seem to come easily to educators at the top of the bureaucratic heap, based on myriad school change initiatives attempted throughout the country in the past two decades. In 1999, the American Institutes for Research, an independent organization based in Washington, D.C., found that only three of the twenty-four education reform models used in more than 8,000 schools across the country could demonstrate a strong positive impact on student achievement.[2] Indeed, most school reforms have not been thoroughly evaluated or sustained.

"Very few have any evidence at all, and especially evidence

that is independent of developers," Herbert J. Walberg, a research professor of education and psychology at the University of Illinois at Chicago, said in an interview with *Education Week.* "This kind of screening would never be acceptable in medicine."[3]

The haphazard implementation of reform explains why so few initiatives survive once the start-up funds dry up and why most haven't spread to other schools and school districts. Educators are part of a system that is almost impervious to radical change; those at the top have little incentive to alter the structure that promoted them, and those at the bottom typically lack the time and the training to carry the reform banner beyond their own hallways. The "trailblazers," educators whom Phillip Schlechty at the Center for Leadership in School Reform describes as the immediate groundbreakers, often get tired and lose interest when so few of their colleagues follow. With obstacles erected by the bureaucratic barons and snares set by those who are too fearful to leave their stakes, these early implementers typically stop in the middle of the journey. Some of them might continue tinkering with the recommended strategies, but by then the project has become so diffuse that no one can say with any certainty whether the original agenda has or might have succeeded.

"If whole-school reforms practiced truth-in-advertising, even the best would carry a warning like this: 'Works if implemented. Implementation variable," Lynn Olson writes in *Education Week.* "Research suggests that if they're well-implemented, some of these designs can produce substantial gains in student achievement. The better the implementation, the better the payoff. But study after study has found that implementation is often problematic and inconsistent, even at school sites that have been identified as exemplars."[4]

Finally, there are the students whom all school reforms target. Will they benefit from the prescribed changes? Will they ever measure up to the nation's elusive standard of academic accomplishment? Or will they continue to fulfill centuries of expectations that some children have what it takes to succeed and others just don't?

"Even if teachers, against considerable odds, were to transform the curriculum they use in their classrooms to bring it into line with a reform effort, there is little to reassure us that the students in those classes would learn what the reform curriculum was supposed to convey," writes David F. Labaree, a Michigan State University education professor and the author of *How to Succeed in School Without Really Learning* and *The Making of an American High School.* "Students, after all, are willful actors who learn only what they choose to learn. Teachers can't make learning happen; they can only create circumstances that are conducive to learning. . . . So this last crucial step in the chain of curriculum reform may be the most difficult one to accomplish in a reliable and predictable manner, since curriculum reform means nothing unless learning undergoes reform as well."[5]

Learning is the only thing that matters in the Jefferson Regional Campus project. And on that scorecard, the statistics are promising but incomplete.

17

GETTING DOWN TO BUSINESS

I n a 1999 article in *Education Week*, reporter Lynn Olson summarized factors that leading researchers believe are critical to the success of school reform. These include strong school leadership; clear and specific designs that the faculty understands and supports; sufficient money and time for the staff to train, plan, and collaborate on instruction; the ability to network with schools undergoing similar transitions; and school district leaders who back the reforms and provide ongoing resources to support them.[1] All of those factors contributed to the development of the Jefferson Regional Campus project, but their presence or absence was especially noteworthy at the business academy, the first of the four planned career academies to open in Gladston. Because the business academy served students who had already begun their high school years in the system the restructuring project aims to fix, it offers a good opportunity to explore the challenge of trying to change course midstream. The lessons from the business academy's first year, therefore, are particularly relevant to organizers who are trying to bring small programs to scale.

In promotional materials distributed to Gladston ninth-graders and their parents in early 1999, the business academy planners said the program would "offer students a new approach to business education. Measuring their progress against challenging and objective standards, students will be introduced to the world of business through projects that inte-grate academic theory and realistic problem solving." Students also were supposed to be able to use state-of-the-art technolo-gy, shadow professionals on the job, and create products that would be evaluated by experienced business experts, as well as by their teachers.

The business academy accepted ninety-eight Jefferson and Lincoln sophomores who expressed an interest in learning about jobs in fields such as accounting, marketing, and information systems. In addition to those three subjects, all students were supposed to take math and English at the business academy, then return to either Jefferson or Lincoln in the afternoon for the remainder of their courses. The plan was to add another grade level to the academy each year until it offered a full com-plement of introductory and advanced business courses to stu-dents in grades ten through twelve.

From the beginning, however, the business academy

seemed to be on shaky ground. Overshadowed by the early excitement over the larger, more heavily promoted freshman academy and subservient to the fractious school system that it was supposed to help change, the business academy never seemed to get much attention or acclaim. From generally uninspiring instruction and reluctant leadership to computers and software that didn't work properly, the business academy suffered from a series of mishaps that frustrated students and teachers alike. Only twenty-three of the original ninety-eight students who signed up for the pilot year chose to return for their junior year. Although some of those decisions were caused by students' changing interests, some students said they might have returned if there had been better curriculum and scheduling coordination between the business academy and Jefferson and Lincoln high schools. For example, the students said the lack of such coordination forced many of them to choose between a college prep *or* business curriculum, with no opportunity to blend the two. As a sophomore named Dremus observed, "I just don't think they were ready" to open the academy.

Dremus, like many of his classmates, was astute enough to notice his teachers' varied enthusiasm and preparation and the way they operated in isolation from their colleagues at Jefferson and Lincoln high school. The five business academy teachers and their instructional leader, Al Gazortz, had participated in several of the training sessions that freshman academy Program Leader Janey Lewis organized for her staff during the summer of 1999, but they did not attend every session. Nor did Gazortz approach his role with gusto, appearing to be uncomfortable displaying the rock-the-boat behavior that leadership often requires. During an interview, Gazortz explained that some of his reluctance stemmed from his disinterest in being the business academy *program* leader; he was interested in the instructional leader's role, which would have allowed him more time in the classroom working with teachers and students. He said the initial business academy plan called for both positions, but the instructional specialist was eliminated in the final stages. As a result, Gazortz kept the title of the job he had lobbied for but also became the de facto program leader, assuming responsibilities he neither wanted nor felt fully capable of fulfilling.

As a twenty-three-year teaching veteran of the Gladston school system, Gazortz felt ill at ease as a change agent in a community that had formed his professional mien. He had been *part* of the system, as were most of his business academy faculty members. And although he acknowledged disagreeing with certain practices within the district, he never had been one to play the role of internal agitator. So rather than imposing tough new demands on his staff during the summer of 1999 and later, when their instructional practices or grading policies began to alienate students and annoy him, Gazortz calmly explained his positions and hoped his colleagues would decide to change on their own.

"I don't like being the heavy," he said. "I like things being done the way they should be."

In school reform, hoping that instruction will happen as planned usually isn't sufficient to make it happen. As researchers noted in the *Education Week* summary of school reform success, moving restructuring initiatives forward requires a vigilant leader who can set clear standards, provide ongoing and focused assistance, and keep the pressure on until the necessary changes occur. Gazortz wasn't interested in those tasks. Consequently, problems persisted rather than abated.

Consider the business academy math classes. Promotional materials promised that "the English and math components...will be flexible so that students may opt for different levels of English or math," but the math teacher was unprepared to work with sophomores whose skills ranged from remedial Math Essentials to Algebra II/Trigonometry. In interviews during the eighth month of school, Algebra II students complained that their math class was the biggest instructional problem at the business academy. (The math classes moved back to the home high schools beginning with the 2000–2001 academic year.) Students with advanced skills said they were frustrated that they had to spend so much time working independently while their teacher tended to the needs of average and struggling students. Gazortz said the academy also offered three levels of English II — regular, college prep, and advanced — but the instructor of that course was better able to adapt lessons to teach all the students in her classroom.

"The Algebra II students, we had to work by ourselves," Dremus said, adding that the lack of challenging instruction had adversely affected his grades.

"I'm normally pretty good at math," said Stephanie, an honors student, "but when we started out the year we just had our books, basically, and the teacher was too busy with the other students and couldn't help us much. So I was really struggling at the beginning and not doing so well."

"I had in Algebra II what I had in Algebra I last year [at Community Catholic High School]," a student named Heather said, rolling her eyes.

For her part, math teacher Darlene Runager thought she was accommodating all the students in her classes. "The…thing I like is not having to move them [the slower students] ahead. I used to have to hold…those who do well back, and now I don't," she said excitedly less than two months into the school year. "I tell them to go ahead, and that makes them feel good."

But Runager was spending so much time working with average and slow students until they grasped concepts that those who were supposed to "go ahead" had to do so without any guidance from her. With just four years of teaching experience, Runager didn't seem to know how to alter her classroom strategies to simultaneously meet the needs of a widely mixed group of students. She had not received much training or coaching about using more innovative approaches, such as developing mini-lessons and varying the complexity of assignments for different learners, which might have helped ease the frustrations of some of her students.

In addition, Runager and Gazortz started the school year

with a strained relationship. From openly arguing about how to group the sophomores so they would not spend all day with the same classmates to clashing over the proposed implementation of block scheduling, the two educators allowed their disagreements and their personality differences to impede professional progress. When students complained about their math classes, Gazortz said, he tried to persuade Runager to make some adjustments and adapt her lessons to meet students' varied ability levels. Nevertheless, the changes she made didn't end the confusion in her classes.

A sophomore named Greg said Runager, apparently trying to connect with students, began spending a lot of class time discussing the trials and triumphs of the Lincoln High School track team, which she coached. When Runager assigned homework problems at the end of the class, Greg said, many students did not understand how to complete them, having spent most of the period talking about sports.

"It's like we're left in the dark," his classmate Ireshia concurred.

Later in the school year, after Gazortz received money from the school district to hire a part-time teacher to separately instruct the students enrolled in Algebra II, the sophomores who remained in Runager's class said she again changed course and pushed them ahead at breakneck speed.

"She should sit down with us and show us how to do it right, because if you see a whole class not do well on a test, that means someone's not teaching right or we're not studying,"

Ireshia said, adding that Runager told students they needed to 'keep going ahead.' "You cannot keep going if I don't know what was shown to me first," Ireshia contested. "I can't add another step if I don't know the first step."

Ireshia didn't make her case to the staff at the business academy, however. Weary of trying to figure out how to succeed in her math class, she became frustrated with and skeptical of the business academy's ability to meet her academic needs. On a more positive note, the Algebra II students applauded Gazortz's intervention and said they were excelling in their new class with the adjunct instructor.

Runager was not the only business academy teacher whom students complained about, nor did her instruction consistently miss the mark. Many days she taught with enthusiasm and energy, and she seemed inspired by her work. But her experience trying to reach students whose academic skills were so varied illustrates one of the difficulties of keeping school change initiatives moving at a steady pace. Many people — in this case, students and teachers — arrive at the starting point having been prepared very differently for the race. Some are ready to proceed at top speeds; others need a more deliberate pace. Shifting from a system that expected only *some* students to succeed to one that expects *all* of them to meet the same high goals requires substantial shifts in attitudes and practices. In the best of circumstances, the transition period will be messy, even more so when teachers are under pressure to show quick and impressive results.

"One of the things I probably dislike about the business

academy is the way that the teachers are in a big hurry," said Mike, a quiet and generally compliant student. "They're afraid they're going to fall behind some of the other classes, and so there's like a test almost every day in some of our classes, and some of them are in just a big hurry to keep up with where the book says they're supposed to be."

Part of the rush to show progress stemmed from the faculty's limited teamwork and planning before the business academy opened, a condition that did not change during the school year. Unlike Lewis at the freshman academy, Gazortz did not engage the ongoing consultation of Judy Hummel from the Center for Leadership in School Reform. Consequently, he and his staff tried to implement the reform in solitude, having no trained professional from the outside offering seasoned perspective. There also were external factors that put the staff in a defensive position. For example, the academy was in a former office building that had to be completely renovated before classes started in August 1999. But, as so often happens with construction projects that are dependent on variables such as government bidding procedures and the availability of equipment, the district couldn't meet the proposed schedule for completion. The business academy opened its doors on the first day of the new school term with temporary furniture, unfinished ceilings and walls, and daily intrusions from construction workers wielding jackhammers and drills. These problems proved distracting, but the delayed installation of cables and wires needed to power the new computers proved debilitating. The academy's much-touted high-technology focus was sidelined for most of the first nine-week grading period. "And when they [the computers] did boot up, they didn't have all the programs the teacher said they needed," Dremus said.

When the computer software finally arrived, information systems teacher Beverly Beasley couldn't get it to load properly. Gazortz said the school district did not respond to his repeated requests for assistance, and district policy prevented him from hiring an outside vendor to troubleshoot the computer snafus. Consequently, the first grading period sailed by while the business academy students sat in classes that were supposed to show them how to use state-of-the-art equipment that they couldn't turn on. All the computers were functioning by the end of the grading period, but the delay meant that Beasley could not adequately assess her students' skills.

"What happened was she extended the first nine-week period," a student named Rocky explained. "For the time being, when the report cards came out, she just gave us incompletes."

Students said their parents became angry when they saw the report cards and accused them of failing to complete the required curriculum because of laziness or disorganization. They refused to believe the verbal and written explanations Beasley sent home. She had acted responsibly, but parents either didn't understand or accept the explanations. In interviews, students acknowledged that the confusion over the first-period grades was beyond the control of Gazortz and Beasley, but they resented being unfairly blamed by their parents.

"When your parents are like mine, they didn't really care what you said," said Mike. "It's more what's on the paper, which wasn't very good…. The teachers try to do their job, but they were made promises [that weren't delivered] and it's really hard for [them]."

Gazortz said the uproar over the nonfunctioning equipment was the most frustrating episode of the business academy's first year. For most of the first semester, he was visibly agitated when he discussed the problems it had caused and worried that the incident might permanently tarnish the academy's reputation.

Gabriel O'Bryan, implementation director for the Jefferson Regional Campus project, agreed that the early technology limitations were difficult, but he offered some perspective a year later.

"They ran into problems they had not anticipated and it was just a circle," he explained, referring to the construction crew and the building planners. "We opened the building too soon. The electricians were to be in three weeks earlier than they did. That threw the technology off, and so that threw everybody off schedule. Technology [staff] had no opportunity to go into the school before school started.

"Being a pilot year last year, we knew we'd run into problems, but there are lots of things we've solved for this year," O'Bryan said, adding that the Jefferson Regional Campus had since hired an on-site technology director, no longer relying on the limited staff at the district offices.

After the frustrations with the technology glitches sub-sided, Gazortz began listening more to students who had other complaints about the business academy. Whether they earned straight A's or struggled in their classes, many of these teenagers shared impressive insights about what worked well and not so well in the Gladston school system. They weren't just venting about problems; as members of the first class to attend the busi-ness academy they felt responsible for helping to shape and improve the pilot program for future students.

Gazortz eventually formed an academic council to give all students an opportunity to speak through a representative group of their classmates. Some of the council's concerns were envi-ronmental in nature, such as a request for a place to hang their coats and the need for waste receptacles inside each bathroom stall. Other issues directly related to curriculum and instruction. Students unanimously praised the small size of the school, strongly encouraged the faculty to continue using block sched-uling, and suggested that teachers modify their heavy use of project-based assignments, which the planners of the Jefferson Regional Campus had embraced.

"One thing I don't like…is all the projects they give us *at once*," Dremus said emphatically. "Like almost *exactly* at the same time. That's too much…that's just crazy."

"Some teachers assign big projects at the same time like they don't know about each other's projects," his classmate, Nikki, observed. "I think they need to talk to each other more."

"I like the idea of projects because that helps you understand the material. But if all you do…is project after project…projects get old after awhile," Heather said. "Some people learn better from projects, but some people learn better from other [sources]."

Halfway through the school year, the business academy switched from five sequential forty-five minute classes daily to extended blocks of ninety-minute classes held on alternate days. Students overwhelmingly liked the new approach.

"One thing I like about the business academy is the block schedule," Dremus said, "because you get like two extra days to do your homework assignment for that one class…. If you had all five of these classes in one day there'd be project after project, and it would stretch you to have it done for a certain time."

"Every time you go to class [at her home high school], you usually do get some type of homework and…if I have homework in five classes there's something that's not going to get done," Heather added. At the business academy "if you have the extra day to do it, you're more likely *to* do it."

Heather also pointed out the benefits of the business academy policy that allowed students to retake tests twice to improve their grades because she said it ensured students would have time to study.

"Usually if you take a test, you study for it and once you take it you just forget about it," her classmate Mike explained. "You study, hope that you pass it, and then forget about it. But here [at the business academy] if you fail, you do it again and you remember more."

Mike offered another reason that the testing policy made sense. "As a student, you get the feeling that teachers care about you because they take the extra time to make sure you know the material and get a good score," he said.

As research from the Search Institute has shown with adolescents nationwide, the two things that students at the business academy repeatedly sought from their teachers were care and challenge. Nearly all students, including those who chose not to return for their junior year, said they received a stronger dose of that formula at the business academy than at either Gladston high school. Many credited the encouragement they received from accounting teacher Bill Gibson, a thirty-two-year veteran of the Gladston school system. A balding, broad-chested man with a booming voice, Gibson is not shy about saying that he prefers traditional teaching methods. But even though he primarily relies on lectures to get his points across and insists that students follow strict decorum in his classes, Gibson is an engaging teacher who looks after each teenager. Throughout the school year, he consistently drew students to him by knowing when to laugh, when to listen, and when to push. He set high expectations for his students, but he made sure that each of them grasped the principles of accounting, often moving around the classroom to work one-on-one with students and always reviewing skills with the entire class.

"The best [class] is accounting because he'll sit down with you and work with you until you get it," Greg said.

Ireshia said Gibson "never says, 'I don't have time' or 'We

have to move on.'"

As Jacinta, another sophomore, said: "He sits there and he helps us, and we don't go on until everyone has everything known to them."

Darius was one student who particularly flourished under Gibson's guidance. At age seven, with one parent dead and the other in prison, Darius went to live with his grandmother. He responded to the disruptions in his life by frequently acting out in school. Teachers put him in special education classes and labeled him "severely behaviorally handicapped." Darius eventually learned to control his behavior, but he fell behind academically and struggled to focus consistently. Gibson looked beyond Darius's troubled past and saw a student with an aptitude for accounting and the ability to pay attention when he was engaged in his work. Encouraged by Darius' interest in the subject, Gibson enlisted him as an unofficial instructional assistant who coached his fellow classmates, particularly with computer applications of the subject.

Gibson reached out to students in other ways. When he realized that some students didn't have access to computers outside of school, he began opening the business academy's computer lab at 6:30 A.M. so they could complete their assignments. The staff had a rule that all papers had to be typed, but many students said they didn't have time to finish their work in class and lacked comparable — or any — computer equipment at home.

"It's just like a big scramble of needing more computer

time," Rocky said.

At first, Gazortz said the business academy staff members couldn't stay long after classes dismissed because they coached athletic teams and had to conduct practices in the afternoon. As a result, no one was available to monitor the building after one-thirty each afternoon. When pressed, however, Gazortz acknowledged that he and a few other teachers could have stayed to help students, but didn't.

For a student such as Rocky, who was taking a full load of classes, working thirty hours outside of school, and participating on the wrestling team at Lincoln High School, the limited computer access at the business academy added a huge burden to his already stressful life. Rocky said he was grateful to Gibson for opening the academy's doors early, and he and several other students routinely walked to school in adverse weather and darkness to use the computers so they could maintain good grades.

During the second semester, Gazortz began using students' suggestions to plan for the 2000–2001 school year. He added a study period because students said they needed more structured time during the day to work with teachers on specific lessons. He also made the environmental improvements students requested, and he formalized the block scheduling they liked so well. Yet, Gazortz and his staff never fully recovered from their slow start. For example, they didn't schedule the job shadowing experiences and business internships they had promised, which further frustrated the students.

"A lot of people in this building can get straight A's, but

they don't have any real-world experience," Darius pointed out. "We need to get out of this building sometime and experience what the real world is about."

Gazortz offered no explanation for why he and his staff had not aggressively pursued such arrangements with local businesses. The few field trips they took to area companies intrigued many students, but they weren't able to take advantage of ongoing programs.

Results from the business academy's first year showed that its passing rate for students was similar to Jefferson and Lincoln high schools. However, the academy did produce better attendance rates and fewer discipline referrals, a sign that certain components of the program were working well. In addition, students said the academy's small size gave them a sense of safety and belonging that was new to their high school experience, and they believed that in general the instruction was better than at the home high schools.

"I think that the setting here, the way they have everything set up, is a good environment. You can learn in it," Rocky said. "You get a lot of tough classes…but you are challenged and if you…want to succeed here then you can."

Janet Moranis, director of instruction for the Jefferson Regional Campus, said many issues contributed to the business academy's first-year problems. "We're a work in progress," she explained. "I like to think of it [the reforms] as if you were doing a home remodeling process, you know, when everything is torn up and you're frustrated but you have to keep your eye on the end goal and what it's going to look like. I guess in my heart that's what I want to believe: that we're a work in progress and we're going to get there over time."

Most of the conditions for success exist in the Jefferson Regional Campus project. For example, Gazortz could exert stronger leadership rather than hoping for improvements among his faculty. Critical to that is requiring their active participation in ongoing professional development that would better prepare them for collaboration and creative teaching techniques. Finally, instead of allowing themselves to be overshadowed by the freshman academy, the business academy faculty could reach out to colleagues across the campus and engage in regular networking sessions that might boost academic achievement throughout the district.

Many business academy students who were part of the pilot year believe in Gazortz's ability to produce deeper changes that might sustain the academy's initial progress. Their confidence gives him a strong foundation on which to build.

18

THE HERO'S JOURNEY

L iterature professor and author Joseph Campbell — whom television commentator Bill Moyer featured in the Public Broadcasting Service special *The Power of Myth* — spent many years documenting the stories that unite generations of people around the world. Campbell asserts that our entire philosophical, spiritual, and artistic history can be linked by some of these common tales and themes. One of the myths, which Campbell calls the journey of the archetypal hero, parallels the process of educational change.

As Campbell explains it, the hero's journey begins when a person decides to venture forth from the common world to the world of wonder. In this almost supernatural sphere, the adventurer encounters forces that seek to thwart his (the heroes that Campbell describes are

always male) progress. The hero must defeat these powerful enemies, thus fulfilling the duties of a hero, and afterward return
home with greater power and knowledge than he had before.

The hero's journey is a trip of transformation, an adventure that enables an ordinary person to become extraordinary. As
Campbell tells us, the hero must go through several stages before
he successfully overcomes all the obstacles placed in the path to
enlightenment. The first stage involves *separation* from the known
world. In this phase, the hero is "drawn into a relationship with
forces that are not rightly understood," Campbell writes in *The
Hero with a Thousand Faces*.[1] Initially, the hero might resist; he is not
always a willing volunteer. But it is this decision to refuse or
accept the challenge that separates the victims from the sur-
vivors.

The second stage is the *initiation* — crossing into the next
world. This phase often includes some sort of supernatural
assistance that, in Campbell's words, "provides the adventurer
with amulets against the dragon forces he is about to pass."[2] In
crossing the threshold, which represents the hero's current life
horizon, the hero agrees to wander into the danger zone, the
unknown. At this juncture, the gods further test the resolve and
the courage of the hero.

The final stage is the *return*, which is indicated by significant changes in the hero's actions and beliefs. By overcoming
conflicts and enduring many trials, the hero has become a sur-
vivor. Successfully navigating the past and the future has helped
the hero establish his place in the present. He has become the

master of that which is both human and devine. Yet, it's not enough for the hero to change himself. He also must share the lessons from the adventure with others, in effect, inspiring them to begin their own journeys of transformation.

"To say that every hero symbolizes all human beings is to say that he symbolizes what all humans want to be, not what they are," Robert A. Segal writes in *Joseph Campbell: An Introduction*. "For in practice few are heroic. All may harbor a deeper side of themselves awaiting discovery, but only a few possess the courage and perseverance to discover it. The hero is heroic exactly because he does what everyone else either will not or cannot do."[3]

If we extend these descriptions to the process of restructuring schools, we see some startling similarities. Here's the most important: For education reform to succeed beyond a single classroom or a single school, many individuals must agree to change their practices, stick with the shifts through the inevitable strains and struggles, then pass on their new knowledge and discoveries to others. Admittedly, it's difficult for educators to think about their larger place in the world when they're knee-deep in student apathy or stuck behind a pile of paperwork designed to feed the bureaucratic beast. But for many, fear gets in the way of even starting an examination of their practices. So, instead of thoroughly evaluating the objectives of education reform and figuring out how to meet the goals, they react like the superstitious villagers in the movie versions of *Dracula*, placing metaphorical rings of garlic around their necks to keep the "monster" away. And therefore, change, the only thing that's really constant in life, becomes the enemy that must be avoided at all costs.

Every day, all across the country, teachers ask children to accompany them on an adventure called learning. But when asked to make their own hero's journey, to move out of their comfort zones to a place of richer understanding and complexity, many teachers venture to the threshold and then turn back because they're too afraid of the demons that might lie ahead.

"We're experts at changing lives," acknowledged John Herzfeld, an award-winning English teacher from Kentucky, "but amateurs at changing our own. We open new ideas to kids, and the world is bigger for them as a result. But we're reluctant to change ourselves because it's so hard, so unpredictable, and so scary. To truly change a society, we need heroes, and to change ourselves, we must become those heroes. We must enter the dark woods, confront the fierce dragon, and finally discover, perhaps to our chagrin, that what had kept us from victory was not the beast without, but the fear within."[4]

As the 2000–2001 school year began in Gladston, fear and its various manifestations gripped many educators by the gullet. But there were also some surprising shifts in attitudes and approaches, suggesting that more educators had or were contemplating embarking on the hero's journey. Reform was starting to seep into the Gladston school district, through both individual initiative and institutional pressure, and those who were affected reacted along an emotional continuum that ranged from anger to confusion to interest. For example, in a two-sided "Special Edition" of the biweekly newsletter distributed from the office of the Gladston Professional Educators Association, President Ted Adams blasted some of the mandated changes and criticized the inadequate training provided to staff members who were being asked to teach and lead differently.

"The frustrations created by not giving the proper training to the individuals charged with making these programs work far over shadow [*sic*] any success they may have," he wrote in an article that carried the headline, Frustration Reigns. "Because of all the grants, program and curriculum changes, we as a school system appear to be focused on *nothing!* Why are not the high school academies up and running at a much greater extent than they are? Where are the buildings for the JRC [Jefferson Regional Campus]? Why has the JRC development seemed to be placed on the back burner?...What are the plans for the freshman academy if 750 students hopefully sign up to attend next year? How are we planning to integrate the positive learning experiences that are occurring daily at our two high schools with the successes we are seeing at the freshman academy? And to what can we actually attribute the success the freshman academy is having?"

In an interview in November 2000, Adams acknowledged that some of his concerns stemmed from the many years that he and other educators had been involved in planning Gladston's school changes, including those that predated the Jefferson Regional Campus project. Additionally, memories of old prob-

lems in the school district had collided with the realities of the
new challenges, which forced his frustrations to spill out into the
open. In the early 1990s, for example, when the Gladston school
district had converted its junior highs to middle schools, teachers who were supposed to serve in the new middle schools had
worked an extra week after the school year ended to learn about
recommended new practices such as teaming. However, he said,
when some teachers took other jobs or retired, their replace-
ments never received any training to help them with successful
middle school practices — and the district had not sponsored
professional development sessions on those topics since then.

"Subsequently you're on a middle school team and supposed to work together, Adams said. "But every time a team
member changes, the complexity of the team changes, and
there's been no ongoing training to deal with that."

At the end of the 1999–2000 school year, Adams said,
elementary teachers in Gladston initially were told that they
could *voluntarily* adopt a method of reading instruction called
four-block scheduling as part of the district's broader restructuring push. When they later discovered that they all would be
required to change, many suspected that the district had fallen
back into its habit of quickly shifting policies and providing
limited professional training.

Chief Education Officer Denise Bannister suggested that
Adams must be mistaken about the intensive literacy focus in
the elementary schools being optional. All teachers were supposed to focus on guided reading, phonics, and writing for nine-

ty minutes each day. "Nobody ever talked about that being voluntary," she said in an interview. "What *is* voluntary is what materials you use in those instructional blocks." Bannister said many teachers talked excitedly about the progress students were making with the consistent emphasis on language development skills. She said the school district also was using a federal grant to pay for a literacy specialist in each elementary school to help train teachers and support their work.

Superintendent Lyndon LaGrange said he believed Adams' newsletter complaints represented the "strong voices of a few" instead of the majority of the district's teachers, but he acknowledged that the sentiments indicated a high degree of stress within the school system.

"I do believe that with any change you have frustrations and, yes, there are frustrations here now," LaGrange said in an interview. "But I don't believe it represents a crisis at this point. What I believe is that it can be reduced through better communications. . . . I am making a more concentrated effort to talk to the various groups."

To that end, Adams said he met with LaGrange, Bannister, and several top administrators to figure out how they could improve the flow of information to and from teachers "so everybody can see how all the pieces fit together." He offered to survey all the district's teachers to find out in great detail what they needed help with and who could provide the assistance. The original planning group then would meet before the end of 2000 to review the responses and figure out how to respond, he said.

"It's a first step, not a cure-all, but an acknowledgement by both sides that we're not communicating well," Adams said. He added that he was pleased that early in the 2000–2001 school year Jefferson and Lincoln staff members had jointly participated in a condensed version of the training that the faculty at the freshman academy had engaged in during the summer of 1999. The teachers' union had supported the school district's successful appeal to the state department of education to use two regularly scheduled school days for the training. "The thing that was most positive in my view is that this is the first time we've gotten Jefferson and Lincoln staffs together," Adams said. "That was a major accomplishment.... I heard a lot of good things about that. People said it was good to be able to talk to colleagues from the other school and other departments."

Adams said he believed teachers had become more open to learning about and spreading the reform initiatives under way, particularly those at the freshman academy, because they had seen some positive results from the practices there. But at the same time, he was concerned that Gladston would be unable to sustain the progress after the Jefferson grant and the state and federal subsidies ended.

"I've expressed the same thing to the superintendent and to Dr. Bannister," Adams said. "We may have through blind luck, but also through a lot of hard work, stumbled on to a key to what's working in the urban school setting." At the freshman academy, "they've got small class sizes, but also different assessments and relationships with kids. They have additional time to work together with teams. All those things together, not any one thing in particular, are producing some very positive results. My frustration is that we can't afford to duplicate those.... When the grants are gone, how do we afford the funding?"

Bannister said she shares Adams' concerns, which is why she asked the Davidson Foundation to let the school system use the balance of the restructuring grant for a fifth year (the $10 million grant originally was to be spread over four years) and why she simultaneously asked the Gladston education partnership to support her plan to seek additional funds from the state by becoming a model for urban school districts. In her report to the Gladston education partnership's board of directors in November 2000, Bannister also said the Gladston school district was seeking additional grants from the federal government under its Small Learning Communities program. She said it was necessary to spread the best practices started in the freshman academy to other schools in the district so students coming into the academy would be better prepared and those leaving the academy could continue their progress.

"I guess it's dramatic in terms of the freshman academy in that they did so many things right," Bannister said, adding that the district's other middle and high schools had not had similar successes with the same students. "So, now we're saying, 'Why is that?'" She said she had begun reviewing achievement data from all the schools after each quarter, instead of waiting until the end of the year, to make adjustments more quickly. She also was insisting that school leaders measure students' achievement gains and behavioral improvements and be able to attribute any changes to specific interventions. The freshman academy has shown that different instruction and relationships are "working for three hundred twenty kids, and now four hundred seventy five. Can we get it to work for one thousand kids? The scaling-up process, that's what's really hard," she said.

To continue the momentum, Bannister began meeting regularly with teacher leaders throughout the district, explaining the reasons for many of the mandated changes and helping individuals understand how their work connected to the entire restructuring project. For example, she helped the freshman academy staff members see that although they might have been uncomfortable expanding so quickly, their progress was forcing educators at the district's middle and high schools to evaluate how they either prepared students for the academy or built on their successes.

Among those most inspired by the demonstrated progress at the freshman academy was Superintendent LaGrange, who said he had "come full circle" in his belief about the need for and the value of school reform in Gladston. "I'm a traditionalist," he said. "I came up from the ranks of teaching and believed that we were working hard for kids and doing the best we could in public education. But over time, I have seen that, and I know it's a cliché, if we continue to do the same things, we'll get the same results, which is a degree of mediocrity in terms of student achievement. And in urban districts, it's not even that, it's poor achievement. I don't fault anyone for that, but we have to change instruction and change the results."

LaGrange credited the Davidson Foundation and the Gladston education partnership for helping the Gladston school district "overcome inertia" by realizing that they had to alter their course in significant ways. "That hasn't always been a welcome push, and it has strained personal relationships," he said, "but overall I believe it was an absolutely necessary force in bringing this reform about."

In the second year of the freshman academy, Program Leader Janey Lewis and Dean of Students Scott Peterson continued to aggressively push staff members to achieve more with their students and to help the academy's ten new teachers reach the same high standards. As she had during the pilot year, Lewis regularly sat in during various teachers' classes, monitoring their instruction and offering ideas for improvement, and Peterson dealt with teachers on improving their classroom management and discipline skills. Both administrators credited science teacher Leticia Herron with diligently working to improve her daily instruction. And Herron discovered that her influence during the pilot year had been stronger than she previously believed. One morning in October 2000 the freshman academy telephone rang. A former student — now a sophomore at the business academy — was calling to explain that she had missed the school bus and wanted to get to class on time.

She asked if one of *her* teachers would drive her to school. Herron, who had taught the girl the previous year, happily obliged. To outsiders, this might sound like an imposition. To educators at the freshman academy, however, it was almost an honor, proof that they had made a lasting connection with a student.

The pilot year's most consistently successful teaching team, DeLora Sims, Andy Hynes, Ellen Jackson, and Doris Eickmeyer, continued making progress, although Eickmeyer left after the first month of school to become the district's social studies curriculum director. During an interview, Eickmeyer said the new job was challenging but she was hopeful that it might help her spread change throughout the district. Eickmeyer's replacement at the freshman academy was first-year teacher Daniel Sutton, whose energy and enthusiasm were well suited to the team.

The departure of Eickmeyer gave Jackson a stronger leadership role. Although she previously had earned the respect of students and colleagues, Jackson often acquiesced to Eickmeyer, the more vocal and assertive of the two. During the second school year, however, Jackson found her voice and deftly led her team through what might have been a trying transition with the loss of a key colleague. Her team was one of two that spent most of the first semester on the second floor of the Jefferson Learning Center, located several blocks away from the freshman academy, a move prompted by the academy's second-year expansion to nearly 500 students. The Jefferson Learning Center classrooms were tiny, the computers were scarce, and the staff office barely accommodated eight teachers' desks. Teachers communicated with those in the freshman academy building through walkie-talkies because three months into the school year, they still did not have access to working phone lines. In addition, they had no administrative support on site and no easy access to Peterson when discipline issues arose.

Jackson acknowledged that the new setup was "terrible," but instead of dwelling on the problems, she encouraged her team and the one led by social studies teacher Trevor Hunter to turn a negative experience into a positive one. Before long, the two groups of teachers realized that their close quarters helped keep discipline referrals to a minimum because there wasn't much room for students to misbehave out of sight of one of the eight faculty members. And with Peterson across campus, the teachers dealt with students' behavioral outbursts head-on. In addition, the teachers started collaborating across teams, taking advantage of their proximity to each other's classrooms. Jackson and Sutton, for example, involved Hunter in a combined literature and civil rights lesson using Maya Angelou's book *I Know Why the Caged Bird Sings*. Jackson invited Hunter to bring his pet parrot to class and talk to students about the characteristics of its species. Students then wrote essays from the point of view of a caged bird. As a bonus, they learned more about a dimension of Hunter outside the classroom.

On another occasion, Jackson and Hunter responded to students' complaints about excessive homework and their burdensome schedules by working with their teammates to conduct an impromptu gripe session for students from both teams. Teachers listened as eighty-odd students crammed into a stuffy classroom and discussed the stress in their lives, ranging from family problems to after-school jobs. As the students' frustrations grew, teachers asked them to begin offering potential solutions, after which they began to understand the challenges of operating a school and trying to address the needs of all students. Moreover, they recognized how important it is to be flexible when you're trying to keep up with the relentless pace of change.

In another case, science teacher Andy Hynes described how he had helped Hunter's students understand the scientific applications of a history lesson because he had overheard the preliminary discussion, having been only three feet across the hall. Hynes credited the spirit of cooperation between the two teams — and their crowded classrooms — for encouraging such impromptu teaching opportunities.

"My favorite part [of the second school year] is coming in and trying to make connections," Hynes said. "It allows them [students] to see me as a multidimensional person, and it helps them see themselves that way, that they can be multidimensional and not so compartmentalized."

Although Hynes' tiny classroom limited his ability to conduct true lab experiments, he relished being so physically close to his students. He laughed as he remembered his frustration with the large and too-highly-traveled science lab at the freshman academy. In contrast to the first year, Hynes was confident and in control of his classes. When disruptions did occur, he easily refocused his students. Because his classroom management skills were so much better, he knew when to let class discussions flow and when to cut them off. During a lesson on speed and velocity, for example, Hynes' students used a remote-powered toy truck with loose objects in the seats to demonstrate sudden impact. The experiment caused students to relate their own experiences with car crashes, and their conversation eventually led to an informal debate about the practicality and constitutionality of seat belt laws. Throughout, Hynes comfortably asked questions to further his students' intellectual explorations.

Asked about the progress he had made as a teacher, Hynes modestly said he hadn't noticed many changes, except that he was enjoying his job more. Lewis and Peterson were far more effusive in their praise. "He has *grown*, and he has impacted his team!" Lewis said enthusiastically.

"It's a night and day difference," acknowledged Peterson. "It was all a matter of self-confidence. He had all the rest of the attributes and beliefs about kids and the academy, and now he commands their attention."

Hunter, too, was having more success during his second year at the academy. Although he had taught for five years before joining the academy staff, Hunter allowed himself to become a frustrated and often subservient member of a troubled team during the pilot year. Lewis, convinced that Hunter had more to offer than he had been willing or able to demonstrate, shuffled the deck during the summer of 2000 and named him the leader of a different team that consisted of two new teachers and one thirty-year veteran. Hunter, buoyed by the new opportunity and his proximity to Jackson and her team, rose to the challenge.

Another teacher who had decided to join others in making the hero's journey was social studies teacher Lars Hennepin. "If I went back to the middle school today...they wouldn't know me," he said, shaking his head in disbelief at how much he had learned since coming to the freshman academy from the middle school where he had worked for more than a decade.

Lewis acknowledged that despite his obvious strengths as a teacher, Hennepin had come to the freshman academy from a very traditional background and "was tied like an umbilical cord to the overhead [projector]." Although he had done well in that setting, she said, he needed to learn how to move students to higher levels of thinking "so they show *you* instead of you them. As much as I love Lars and I do, I still have to push him."

Spurred by Lewis' constant coaching and the high energy level of two new teachers on his team, Hennepin began to alter his instruction to include a more project-based focus. He was enjoying collaborating with first-year English teacher Jean Yamaguchi, who taught Hennepin to appreciate the connections between literature and history. He, in turn, showed her and math teacher Rose Riordan how to navigate the political waters of the school system and, in so doing, abdicated his former role as the class clown for a more mature leadership position.

Another significant change during the freshman academy's second year was the addition of math as a full credit course. During the pilot year, students had taken math at their home high schools; the math lessons at the academy were designed to reinforce scientific concepts. During the second year, freshman academy teachers not only would teach a full credit math course, but would also play a key role in implementing Bannister's directive to get rid of low-level courses. Beginning with the 2001–2002 school year, Gladston high schools would no longer offer pre-algebra to freshmen. Bannister's plan was to improve the academic progress of Gladston students by aggressively raising the standards. Teachers understood her goal but knew there were practical issues to consider, specifically that too many Gladston students simply were not ready to grasp algebra when they entered high school. To prepare for this transition, freshman academy math teachers DeLora Sims and Barbara Issing investigated various curriculum models before choosing two to try during the second year.

They selected one model that combines algebra and geometry concepts and another that includes a computer tutorial, which enables students to move ahead at their own pace without holding back classmates who are progressing more quickly. Issing, Sims, and their math colleagues at the freshman academy received several days of training on the two models before the school year began. The district planned to spread the training to other teachers at Jefferson and Lincoln high schools before the start of the following school year so students could continue their progress.

Sims said that she was enjoying teaching a class that the students took more seriously because of the accompanying credit but that, as a result, it was more challenging for her to figure out how to integrate math lessons with what the students were learning in science. Ironically, it was Hynes who now sat in on her classes, as she often had done for him during the pilot year, helping to make connections and keep students focused. One student, sitting alone in Sims' math class one afternoon, beamed as he saw Hynes walk through the door.

"Hey, Mr. Hynes! Guess what? I did my homework!" the boy blurted out. The two shared the thumbs-up sign and a smile; the boy had found a positive male role model in Hynes, who had been hungry for the honor.

The most obvious beneficiary of the new math focus was Gary Rosenberger, who had resented not having what he considered an integral role at the freshman academy during the first year. Rosenberger now walked the academy hallways with a bounce in his step, and he beamed as he talked about teaching in collaboration with math teachers Issing, Sims, Kyran Larkin, and Gina Cousens. "I love it," Rosenberger said, a wide grin replacing his typically serious expression. "I get to do more.... I get to help."

Technology teacher Clyde Dalyrymple was as dispirited as Rosenberger was ecstatic. His subject, offered as a full-credit course during the freshman academy's pilot year, took a supporting role during the second year because of the academy's added math credit. The revised plan called for Dalyrymple to offer support to teachers who wanted to incorporate technology into their lessons.

"It was not to remove the impact of technology or our kids learning the skills, but that…it [technology] would be embedded in the other courses," Lewis explained. "It was really going to become the way of doing things."

But with no scheduled daily classes to teach, Dalyrymple didn't think the plan was working. He claimed that few teachers had accepted his offer to help. And because he had served on the planning committee for the academy, he believed that the original intent of the school — to serve as a high-tech center — was being sidelined. In addition, having given up coaching opportunities to spend more time with freshman academy students, Dalyrymple was not only bored, he was angry.

"I'm disappointed that the teachers aren't taking advantage of it [access to the technology lab]," Dalyrymple said. "When things get challenging, people revert back to what's easy." He said he had watched as a teacher showed her students how to use word processing to compile lab data, and "she taught it wrong." In that teacher's defense, however, several colleagues said Dalyrymple's communications skills alienated and ultimately prevented them from voluntarily collaborating with him. He widely distributed a seventeen-page document containing addresses and descriptions of different Internet sites that teachers could use with their classes, but some teachers thought the tone of the document was condescending and chose not to respond to his offer of help.

Dalyrymple credited special education teacher Margaret Tichenor, a new addition to the academy faculty, with bringing her students to the technology lab and collaborating with him. He said Tichenor's students created pie charts representing the percentages of athletes who competed for different countries during the Olympics and calculated the percentage of medals won by each country. Tichenor's students also started a mock business during another class and used computers to produce the invoices.

"These are kids everybody else has given up on, and they were engaged," Dalyrymple said. "It was so neat. They just loved it. They had a piece of paper they had created."

With no set classes and, therefore, no students to connect with on a regular basis, Dalyrymple turned his attentions to Sunset School, which he supervised whenever possible. "I think I've connected with some kids in Sunset School. I really have," he said. "I just think these kids are being shortchanged because I'm not able to teach these kids skills that will make them employable after graduating from high school."

It wasn't the lack of a technology credit that bothered Scott Peterson, although he considered it unfortunate that students had lost something that offered so many of them a different way to appreciate learning. His weariness stemmed from frustration that the faculty was not developing the level of engaging, high-quality work that he expected. Moreover, he was battling many of the same problems of the first year but in greater numbers. The second year was "much harder" than the first, he said, because in addition to advising a larger number of students, he discovered that more of them had greater personal problems that interfered with their learning. During an interview in October 2000, Peterson sat at his desk, welcoming as usual, but keeping one eye on the conversation and the other on the office door, as if expecting a crisis to erupt at any moment.

"We've got more things in place, operationally, procedures, than we did last year, so we're not having to work as hard [in that way]," he explained. "But with kids, I'm frustrated that we aren't doing more. You get bogged down day after day with the same issues, teacher issues, so, you know, we just keep plugging away."

Peterson said Lewis had suggested that he cut back on his hours and let teachers handle more of the discipline problems on their teams. Guidance counselor Mimi Cantrell tried to do her part by recruiting faculty members to teach "enrichment" classes after school on Wednesdays for interested freshmen. The classes included scrapbook-making, a running club and, of course, a basketball session led by Peterson.

In addition to the enrichment basketball class, which was coeducational, Peterson continued his Saturday morning pickup games and added a special Wednesday night session in the Jefferson High School gym for some of the students who had attended the freshman academy the year before. The first weekly session drew seven boys, including Zack, Edward, and Michael, some of Peterson's most frequent "customers" during their freshman year in school. Now they were engaged in a competitive but fun game with their friend and mentor who continued showing them by example how to be a good man. Their ninety-minute exercise session was so spirited that even the most sedentary adult would consider trading couch potato status for a chance to make an alley-oop shot. But additional adults weren't invited. This session was for Peterson's boys, those almost dropouts and delinquents who had started walking with him on the hero's journey and were already better for the adventure.

Zack, the formerly sullen and explosive student, now approached adults with an outstretched hand and a ready smile. He was earning mostly A's in his classes at Jefferson High School, but continued to visit Peterson each morning and during his lunch periods for moral support. Peterson, who said he had spent significant time with Zack during the summer, was clearly delighted by his progress.

"He recently offered to do speaking engagements for the freshman academy if we need to talk to eighth-graders," Peterson said, smiling in amazement. "And he's only had one in-school suspension this year [at Jefferson]."

Zack's former teachers noticed the changes, too. Math teacher DeLora Sims said she had wondered whether Peterson had expended too much energy on Zack during the first year, but the boy's progress had changed her mind. "I'm so glad he [Peterson] is there for him because if he wasn't, who would be?" Sims said.

Michael also credited the freshman academy faculty for helping turn his life around. Michael has supportive parents, and he is a polite teen with an infectious smile, but he struggled academically in middle school and admits that he did not always try to perform well as a freshman. During the fall of his sophomore year at Jefferson High School, however, Michael beamed as he told of earning mostly A's and B's on his first report card.

"I've stepped up to the plate," he said, crediting his academic and behavioral growth to the freshman academy. At the same time, he said, "I miss my teachers." He continues to visit his freshman academy team of Hennepin, Stan Lerner, Megan Short, and Preston Reed at least weekly. "They taught me responsibility, self-control, and determination." And, he said, Peterson had taught him that a basketball gym is a better place to release stress than the classroom.

Edward also was doing well as a sophomore at Jefferson High School, keeping his grades high enough to stay on the varsity basketball team, a goal that Peterson had encouraged him to set the year before. Edward said he missed the close-knit environment of the freshman academy, the project-based learning, and the ready access to technology that he had enjoyed there. He wistfully remembered "the way if you didn't get something, you could ask the teachers and they would stay after school and help you. Here [at Jefferson] they say, 'You need to get a tutor.'"

As these students suggested, the freshman academy had demonstrated that progress is possible with hard-to-reach teenagers — and skeptical adults. Teachers who rarely had ventured from behind the classroom podium now regularly shared ideas and instruction with colleagues and tried to understand students on a more personal level. Students who once feared or taunted their teachers now trusted them enough to learn and behave in ways that made it possible for them to mentor others. The challenge was spreading these practices and strong relationships to the rest of the school system.

In an encouraging sign, Jefferson High School Principal Angelo Hancock had started the 2000–2001 school year by asking Peterson to help him train his staff to use the discipline procedures that had been so successful at the freshman academy. Hancock also began requiring the leaders of each department at Jefferson to conduct monthly planning meetings, much to the pleasure of chemistry teacher Patrick Alton.

"It's a chance to get together...to talk about...our department instead of just attendance and supplies," Alton said approvingly. "I like to meet with other teachers because they have ideas that I don't."

Alton also was delighted that Mary James Decker, his former science colleague at Jefferson, had been named chairwoman of the engineering and technology academy when Regina Crews moved to another leadership position within the Jefferson Regional Campus structure. Alton said he had told Decker he wanted to work with her at the new academy, which is scheduled to begin offering classes in the 2001–2002 school year, if she needed a chemistry teacher.

"I've seen the good effects of teachers working on teams and the sense of community with students," he explained. "I know that sounds cliché-ish, but it's true."

Jefferson math teacher Leslie Newton said she wasn't eager to join one of the academies but was intrigued by their access to technology and the money spent on "teachers and teaching tools." A self-described traditionalist who enjoyed the current structure at Jefferson High School, Newton said that although she wasn't seeking change, she would "go with the flow" when reform moved in her direction. But nearly two decades in the Gladston schools had made her skeptical of whether she and her colleagues would receive sufficient and ongoing professional development to make new teaching methodologies work.

"Come in and show me how to do it," she said. "Don't just tell me."

At the business academy, instructional leader Al Gazortz had begun to move his program forward and said he was "more comfortable" during the second school year. He was visibly relaxed during conversations. And as he conducted a fall staff meeting, Gazortz showed a new assertiveness with teachers while they discussed concerns about students' computer skills and possible changes he wanted to make to their class schedule. He said that he had begun requiring his teachers to accept the responsibility for calling students' parents to help curb truancy and academic delinquency and that he and the faculty were making plans to begin apprenticeship programs for students specializing in business administration and marketing. Indeed, they already had forged a relationship with a large regional insurance company that had agreed to let students regularly visit their employees at the workplace. Gazortz said some of the business academy's second-year improvements were a credit to the maturity of the students, perhaps a nod to the freshman academy, which produced more than one-third of the sophomores attending the business academy for the 2000–2001 school year.

"That's enough to influence other students," he said, explaining that students who entered the business academy during its pilot year had never been exposed to an academic environment that asked them to play an integral role in their learning. As a result, helping students overcome that learning curve delayed the first-year progress of his staff.

During a reflective moment, Gazortz attributed his growth as an administrator to additional training during the summer of 2000 and to a new supervisor, Melinda Rausch, the director of Career and Technical Education for the Gladston school district. Rausch also serves as the chairwoman of the Jefferson Regional Campus project design team. In that capacity, she acts as a liaison between the academy program leaders and the Jefferson Regional Campus office, specifically Chief Education Officer Bannister. Rausch said her primary challenge is to help the career academy program leaders "understand the many ways their programs link to each other and to Jefferson and Lincoln [high schools]." For example, she is working with others to improve curriculum and planning so students who want to continue at the business academy are not shut out because of conflicting course schedules with their home high schools, as happened at the end of the pilot year.

Gazortz said he was delighted to begin reporting to

Rausch, whose teaching background is similar to his own. Until Rausch's appointment in the spring of 2000, Gazortz said he spent much of the pilot year overburdened by the administrative duties of his job and had no direct contact with a supervisor. He also felt somewhat isolated from the rest of the Jefferson Regional Campus developments and lacked a clear sense of direction, later admitting that he occasionally wondered whether he might be a better "number two man." During the second school year, Gazortz began to gain confidence in his leadership. Working with Rausch, he said, has "helped because I have someone I trust, somebody to talk to and who can counsel me. I like the challenges of this job now," he added, saying he had realized that "the old way of doing things was rote."

These changes in attitude among Gladston's educators were hopeful signs for a school system that has enjoyed few opportunities for optimism in recent years. As difficult as those transformations have been, however, greater challenges lie ahead. Sustaining school reform initiatives past the pilot stage continues to be one of the toughest jobs in public education. Changes in leadership, inconsistent financial support, and the public's impatience with the slow results of school reform continue to keep restructuring efforts from firmly taking root in communities nationwide. As Ellen Condliffe Lagemann, an education historian and the president of the Chicago-based Spencer Foundation said during a recent national gathering of the Grantmakers for Education: "When one looks at the history of philanthropy in education, one is hard pressed to come up with projects that have had enduring success."[5]

Research suggests that education reformers need at least five years to make a positive, sustainable impact on student achievement, assuming stable leadership and an absence of major calamities. In Gladston, with Superintendent Lyndon LaGrange nearing his announced retirement, some experienced and knowledgeable members of the local school board considering following suit, and Bannister almost halfway through her four-year contract, the long-term success of the Jefferson Regional Campus project is difficult to predict.

Freshman academy Program Leader Janey Lewis was as resolute as ever in moving forward with the reform model that she had helped start, and she had recruited a growing army of supportive educators along the way. Likewise, despite the frequent friction between her office and teachers in the trenches, Bannister was not backing down from the challenge either. Saying she was pleased to discover that so many people in Gladston care deeply about the community's children and want to make a difference in their lives, she intended to capitalize on that strength by focusing their goodwill toward raising student achievement.

If they collectively succeed, if Gladston does indeed rally to the cause of school change, then the hero that Joseph Campbell credited with enlightenment may truly be said to wear a thousand faces.

ENDNOTES

Chapter 1

[1] David L. Angus and Jeffrey E. Mirel, *The Failed Promise of the American High School 1890–1995*, Teachers College Press, Columbia University, New York, 1999, p. 70.

[2] Ibid, p. 104.

[3] Ibid, p. 103.

Chapter 2

[1] Joetta L. Sack, "Riley Says It's Time to Rethink High Schools," *Education Week*, September 22, 1999, p. 20.

[2] Angus and Mirel, *The Failed Promise of the American High School*, p. 201.

[3] *The Condition of Education 2000*, National Center for Education Statistics, U.S. Department of Education, Washington, DC, June 2000, pp. 167, 171.

[4] "Urban Schools: The Challenge and Location of Poverty," National Center for Education Statistics, U.S. Department of Education, July 1996, p. 118.

[5] Kati Haycock, "Good Teaching Matters…A Lot," *Thinking K–12*, a publication of The Education Trust, Summer 1998, p. 4.

[6] Linda Darling-Hammond, "Teacher Quality and Student Achievement: A Review of State Policy Evidence," Education Policy Analysis Archives, January 1, 2000, Vol. 8, No. 1.

Chapter 3

[1] Marlene Lozada, "A Model Reform," *Vocational Education Journal*, November/December 1995, pp. 30–32.

[2] "Career Academies Rise Above Other Training, Study Says," *Vocational Training News*, June 13, 1996, p. 5.

[3] Robert Evans, *The Human Side of School Change: Reform, Resistance, and the Real-Life Problems of Innovation*, Jossey-Bass Publishers, San Francisco, 1996, p. 4.

Chapter 4

[1] Lorraine Monroe, "The Principal as Educational Leader," *Basic Education*, the Council for Basic Education, Washington, DC, Vol. 44, No. 4, December 1999, p. 3.

Chapter 5

1. "Teacher Quality: A Report on the Preparation and Qualifications of Public School Teachers," U.S. Department of Education, Office of Educational Research and Improvement, Washington, DC, January 1999, pp. v, 47, 48, vi.

2. Andreae Downs, "The Quest for Quality: Schools Seek Teachers Who Shine," *Middle Ground*, National Middle School Association, Columbus, OH, August 2000, p. 10.

3. "Teacher Quality," p. 31.

4. Ibid, p. 11.

Chapter 6

1. Simon Hole and Grace Hall McEntee, "Reflection Is at the Heart of Practice," *Educational Leadership*, May 1999, Vol. 56, No. 8, pp. 34–35.

Chapter 7

1. Jean Johnson and Steve Farkas, "Getting By: What American Teenagers Really Think About Their Schools," a report from Public Agenda, New York, 1997, pp. 26–27.

Chapter 8

1. Johnson and Farkas, "Getting By: What American Teenagers Really Think About Their Schools," pp. 22, 27.

2. "Answers in the Tool Box: Academic Intensity, Attendance Patterns, and Bachelor's Degree Attainment," a report from the U.S. Department of Education, Office of Educational Research and Improvement, June 1999, pp. vi–vii.

3. "Actions for Communities and States," *Thinking K–16*, a publication of The Education Trust, Vol. 3, Issue 2, Fall 1999, p. 29.

4. "Ticket to Nowhere," *Thinking K–16*, a publication of The Education Trust, Vol. 3, Issue 2, Fall 1999, p. 2.

Chapter 9

1. Michael Fullan, *Change Forces: Probing the Depths of Educational Reform*, The Falmer Press, Bristol, PA, 1993, p. ix.

2. Phillip C. Schlechty, "On the Frontier of School Reform with Trailblazers, Pioneers, and Settlers," *Journal of Staff Development*, Fall 1993, Vol. 14, No. 4, p. 49.

3. Ibid. p. 50.

⁴ "Working on the Work Design Qualities Summary," a product of the Center for Leadership in School Reform as presented during training for the Jefferson Regional Campus, July 1999.

Chapter 10

¹ Patricia Wasley, "Teaching Worth Celebrating," *Educational Leadership*, Vol. 56, No. 8, May 1999, p. 9.

² Letter from Judy Hummel to freshman academy staff, May 12, 2000.

Chapter 11

¹ Peter Scales and N. Leffert, Developmental Assets: A synthesis of the scientific research on adolescent development, Search Institute, Minneapolis, 1999.

² Neal Starkman, Peter Scales, and Clay Roberts, *Great Places to Learn: How Asset-Building Schools Help Students Succeed*, , Search Institute, Minneapolis, 1999, p. 39.

³ Ibid.

⁴ Ibid, pp. vii–viii.

Chapter 15

¹ Robert Evans, *The Human Side of School Change: Reform, Resistance, and the Real-Life Problems of Innovation*, Jossey-Bass Publishers, San Francisco, 1996, pp. 235–236.

² Peter C. Scales, "Care and Challenge: The Sources of Student Success," *Middle Ground*, National Middle School Association, October 1999, pp. 21–23.

Chapter 16

¹ Kathleen Kennedy Manzo, "Algebra Benefits All Students, Study Finds," *Education Week*, November 15, 2000, p. 8.

² "Reform programs earn mixed reviews," *The American School Board Journal*, April 1999, p. 14.

³ Debra Viadero, "Who's In, Who's Out: Grant Program's List of 17 Reform Models Attracts Criticism," *Education Week*, January 20, 1999, p. 11.

⁴ Lynn Olson, "Following the Plan," *Education Week*, April 14, 1999, p. 28.

⁵ David F. Labaree, "The Chronic Failure of Curriculum Reform," *Education Week*, May 19, 1999, p. 44.

Chapter 17

¹ Lynn Olson, "Key Ingredients in the Reform Recipe," *Education Week*, April 14, 1999, p. 32.

Chapter 18

[1] Joseph Campbell, *The Hero with a Thousand Faces*, Princeton University Press, Princeton, NJ, 1972, p. 51.

[2] Ibid, p. 69.

[3] Robert A. Segal, *Joseph Campbell: An Introduction*, Penguin Books, USA, New York, 1990, p. 36.

[4] Interview with the authors, November 1, 1998.

[5] Catherine Gewertz, "Foundations Ponder Their Impact on Schools," *Education Week*, November 15, 2000, p. 10.